THE SECRET

Candlestick Charting

Strategies for Trading the Australian Markets

Louise Bedford

Wrightbooks

Also by Louise Bedford
The Secret of Writing Options
Trading Secrets
Charting Secrets

First published in 2000 by Wrightbooks
an imprint of John Wiley & Sons Australia, Ltd
42 McDougall Street, Milton Qld 4064

Office also in Melbourne

Reprinted 2001, 2003, 2004, 2005, 2006, 2007 and 2008

Typeset in Garnet 11.5/13.2

© Louise Bedford 2005

The moral rights of the author have been asserted

National Library of Australia Cataloguing-in-Publication data

Bedford, Louise.
The secret of candlestick charting: strategies for trading the Australian markets.

Includes index.
ISBN: 1 876627 28 X.

1. Stocks - Prices - Australia - Charts, diagrams, etc.
2. Commodity exchanges - Charts, diagrams, etc.
3. Speculation - Australia.
4. Stock price forecasting.
5. Securities - Australia.
I. Title.

332.632280994

All rights reserved. Except as permitted under the *Australian Copyright Act 1968* (for example, a fair dealing for the purposes of study, research, criticism or review), no part of this book may be reproduced, stored in a retrieval system, communicated or transmitted in any form or by any means without prior written permission. All inquiries should be made to the publisher at the address above.

Cover design by Rob Cowpe

Printed in Australia by McPherson's Printing Group

10 9

Disclaimer
The material in this publication is of the nature of general comment only, and neither purports nor intends to be advice. Readers should not act on the basis of any matter in this publication without considering (and if appropriate taking) professional advice with due regard to their own particular circumstances. The author and publisher expressly disclaim all and any liability to any person, whether a purchaser of this publication or not, in respect of anything and of the consequences of anything done or omitted to be done by any such person in reliance, whether in whole or in part, upon the whole or any part of the contents of this publication.

TABLE OF CONTENTS

		Page
Part I — Candlestick Pattern Secrets		
1.	Let's Get Started	3
2.	Single-Line Candle Reversal Patterns	21
3.	Two-Line Candle Reversal Patterns	41
4.	Three-Line Candle Reversal Patterns	62
5.	Trading Concepts and Continuation Patterns	76
Part II — Analysis Secrets		
6.	Candles and Gaps	93
7.	Support and Resistance	100
8.	Western Techniques and Candles	117
9.	Share Stages	131
Part III — Trading Secrets		
10.	A Kindred Spirit	153
11.	Seven Golden Candlestick Rules	161
	Further Reading	165
	Glossary	166
	Index	173

CANDLESTICK TABLE OF CONTENTS

(T) indicates a Top Reversal Pattern.
(B) indicates a Bottom Reversal Pattern.
(C) indicates a Continuation Pattern.
A blank (—) indicates a particular type of candle
that does not form a continuation or reversal by itself.

Candlestick Pattern	**Pattern Implication**	**Page**
The White Candle	—	12
The Black Candle	—	13
Shooting Star	(T)	23

Candlestick Table of Contents (Cont'd)

Candlestick Pattern	Pattern Implication	Page
Hammer	(B)	26
Inverted Hammer	(B)	27
Hanging Man	(T)	29
Doji	(T) & (B)	30
Spinning Top	(T) & (B)	33
Marubozu or Shaven Candle	—	33
Short Candle	—	34
Long and Dominant Candle	—	34
Bearish Rejection	(T)	36
Bullish Rejection	(B)	37
Bearish Engulfing Pattern	(T)	43
Bullish Engulfing Pattern	(B)	45
Dark Cloud Cover	(T)	49
Piercing Pattern	(B)	50
Harami	(T) & (B)	52
Harami Cross	(T) & (B)	54
Evening Star	(T)	63
Morning Star	(B)	66
Evening Doji Star	(T)	68
Morning Doji Star	(B)	68
Two Crows	(T)	71
Upside Tasuki Gap	(C)	82
Downside Tasuki Gap	(C)	83
Rising Three Method	(C)	84
Falling Three Method	(C)	87
Tweezer Top	(T) & (C)	103
Tweezer Bottom	(B) & (C)	107
Upthrusts	(T)	109
Springs	(B)	110
Dominant White Candle	—	110
Dominant Black Candle	—	112

ACKNOWLEDGMENTS

The generosity of significant players in the market never ceases to amaze me! In particular Daniel Gramza, Martin Pring, David Chia, Harry Stanton and Chris Tate (www.artoftrading.com.au) have been incredibly supportive and offered practical advice and suggestions for putting together this publication. All of these men have already established outstanding reputations in the trading industry, so they have very little to gain by being interviewed for this book, or offering an appropriate word of encouragement. Their support has refreshed my view of human nature!

Gary Stone and the team at ShareFinder Investment Services supplied the Market Master software that I used to create the charts in Chapter 8. Gary's knowledge of the relative strength comparison and the SIROC indicator has greatly assisted my own trading results. ShareFinder can be contacted at PO Box 7374, Beaumaris, Victoria, 3193. Ph: 1300 STOCKS. You can access a free demonstration disk of Market Master software by referring to www.sharefinder.com.au.

Chris Bedford, my husband, edited and corrected much of the finer detail of this book. His patience is greatly appreciated.

Thanks to The Trading Game Pty Ltd for providing the data required to create the charts throughout this publication. For more information about data, share trading, training and education, refer to www.tradinggame.com.au.

For more information about candlestick charting, please refer to my website www.tradingsecrets.com.au.

PART I

CANDLESTICK PATTERN SECRETS

Chapter 1
LET'S GET STARTED

Have you ever seen one of those 'magic eye' computer-generated three-dimensional pictures? At first glance it seems to be one-dimensional and quite flat in appearance. However, when you squint and stare at the picture for long enough, an incredible three-dimensional object reveals itself in vivid detail! "Oh, I can see it! It's a space ship with little aliens inside…it's amazing," you exclaim, while the poor person beside you says dejectedly, "Where? Where? I can't see a thing…"

Once you know the trick of seeing the images, all of a sudden you can see them easily and everywhere, much to the frustration of your less-enlightened friends. The method of accessing the hidden image is almost impossible to explain until you can do it yourself.

Candlestick charting is very similar. Once you can see the information in the chart, you will probably never want to look at another type of chart again. You will excitedly talk about 'dark cloud cover' and 'raindrops' until your friends begin to think that you have taken a second job at the weather bureau.

You are about to discover a technique that has the potential to completely alter the way you view charting, yet is complementary to all of the other methods of technical analysis you might use. Technical analysis is defined as the examination of price and volume action on a chart. I predominantly use technical indicators to reach conclusions about the likely direction of share price activity, rather than relying on fundamental data (e.g. balance sheet items such as profit and loss).

Candlesticks form an integral part of my trading activities. If you would like a powerful technique that can pinpoint trend changes prior to many other indicators, show you when a trend is likely to continue and add depth to your existing trading techniques that you never believed would be possible, then candlestick charting is for you.

I have personally found candles to be an invaluable analytical tool. In fact, if all of the technical analysis techniques that I use were forcibly taken away from me due to some bizarre twist of fate, and I had to choose only one to assist in my trading efforts, I would choose the candlestick! Luckily though, I can use the candlestick alongside all of my other favourite analytical methods.

Many advanced traders have developed a high level of sophistication using candlestick analysis. Novice traders will also be greatly assisted by learning about candlestick pattern recognition techniques. Wherever your skills lie on the trading scale from beginner to advanced, the candlestick offers the promise of enhancing your profit potential.

WHY USE CANDLESTICKS?

The visual display of a candlestick chart provides a valuable method of analysing price information. As you attune your eye to candlestick patterns, signals will practically jump off the chart and wrestle you to the ground. You have everything to gain and nothing to lose by using candlesticks, because all of the information in a standard bar chart is already included in a candle chart—it is just represented in a different graphical format. Personally, I always choose candlestick charts in preference to any other chart format because of the depth of information that they present.

An advantage of candlestick charts, compared to standard bar charts, is the level and variety of reversal and continuation patterns that these charts reveal. The majority of these patterns are unique to candlestick charting and are not available by using any other method.

By understanding the psychology behind each pattern, you can reach into the heart of a candle and determine its probable impact on share price action. If you understand the psychological principles driving the creation of a candlestick, you are more likely to understand its potential impact. This skill can be generalised to any new candlestick pattern that you may come across in the future.

There is a continual tug of war in the market, which displays an imbalance of buyer and seller pressure. Whenever a market is in a state of imbalance, the prices will reflect either a bullish or a bearish sentiment. If the market was in perfect agreement about the price a share should be, there would not be any movement in the share price throughout that session. This is a generic principle whether discussing shares, options, warrants, futures or any other market-driven instrument. For this reason, the patterns that are generated by the candles are applicable across any market. This can only add to the widespread acceptance of candlesticks in Western markets in the future. Once you have completed this book, you will be able to use these methods to trade in any market, whether you prefer to trade shares, derivatives or futures. For the sake of simplicity, however, I will predominantly refer to trading shares for examples throughout the book.

> "...the patterns that are generated by the candles are applicable across any market."

There are several candlestick patterns that suggest a trend reversal is imminent, and others designed to imply trend continuation. I'll show you each of the patterns that I use, and provide you with many opportunities to recognise and practise your newfound skills. By taking the time to understand each concept before you continue reading, and completing the exercises available, you will learn the secrets of using candlesticks.

A QUICK HISTORY LESSON

From 1500 to 1600, Japan was a country constantly at war. Military confrontation had become a way of life as feudal lords fought to control rival territories. This period of time became known as 'Sengoku Jidai' or 'The Age of War'. This helps to explain why many candlestick terms have military connotations.

Over a period of 40 years, three charismatic generals—Nobunga Oda, Hideyoshi Toyotomi and Leyasu Tokagawa—unified Japan. Once relative peace had been established, several new opportunities for expansion developed.

It was during this time that the concept of the Japanese candlestick was being explored and used in the rice markets. Because there was no standardised currency, rice became the predominant medium of exchange. In the late 1600s the Rice Exchange was formed to regulate trading proceedings. By 1710 there were more than 1,300 rice dealers. Rather than just deal in actual rice, rice coupons were issued, and these became one of the first forms of futures contracts ever traded. (The 'Tulipomania' that swept the Netherlands in the early 1600s also involved a form of futures contract. During this period in the Netherlands, tulips became the standard medium for exchange and became even more valuable than gold. So, even though we think of ourselves as sophisticated modern traders, many of the basic concepts behind the instruments that we trade today had their origins hundreds of years ago.)

The popularity of these rice coupons in Japan was significant. A 'bale' of rice was the standard amount to be traded. By 1749 there were 110,000 bales of rice traded via 'empty rice coupons' (where the rice was not in physical possession), even though it is estimated that there were actually only 30,000 bales in all of Japan.

In 1724, Munehisa Homma was born into a wealthy farming family. Homma had an aptitude for business and he ultimately became a dominant trader in the Japanese rice market. Although candlesticks were not actually developed by Homma, he studied the psychology of investors and formulated several key trading principles. These concepts eventually evolved into the candlestick charting techniques that we know today.

Candlestick charts were, of course, originally plotted painstakingly by hand. This labour-intensive step, as well as the fact that many Japanese traders could not release their trading methods due to language barriers, meant that the use of the candle was not widespread until recent times. It is only since the early 1990s that candlesticks were discussed in Australian trading circles without the audience

...Business is war..." expecting a follow-up discussion on macramé and knitting lessons! (After I told my friends that I was interested in candlesticks, some were convinced that I had a penchant for handicrafts!) Luckily, candlesticks are now included in the majority of charting packages as a standard method of analysis, alongside the more traditional bar charts and line charts.

A Japanese mentor of mine from the corporate world has two favourite sayings: "Business is war" and "Know your enemy like your brother". Competition and future product developments were all viewed in the light of this philosophy. The 'war' in the case of the trading world is between the bulls and the bears. To 'know your enemy' you must understand the psychological principles that the other side is subject to. Studying candlesticks provides an opportunity to get inside the mind of other traders and to use this exclusive knowledge to develop advanced analytical skills. Hopefully you will also learn how to handle your own emotions while trading.

Today in Japan, it is incredibly rare to find an analyst who consistently views bar charts. The candlestick is the predominant graphic layout, just as the bar chart is for traders in Western society.

READING GUIDE

While you are reviewing the charts in this book, you may see some patterns that I have not labelled. This will occur with increasing regularity as you begin to recognise more and more candlestick patterns. To get the most out of this book, take notes and mark the charts as you see fit. This will assist in your candlestick recognition ability, as well as reinforcing many of the principles that we will be discussing.

Do not let the age of the chart influence your analysis and understanding about the essential principles. The lessons contained in these charts are timeless. Each chart is depicted for the purpose of providing a deeper explanation than you could derive from a purely theoretical approach.

Be aware that some candlestick patterns may not be perfectly formed according to the exact definition, but the impact of these candlesticks may still be relevant. The patterns do not have to look precisely the same as they do in the figures to provide a valid signal. There is some level of subjectivity in defining candlestick patterns, as there is with all technical analysis techniques. For this reason it is appropriate to consider the recognition suggestions for candlestick patterns as 'guidelines' instead of 'rules'. I will indicate when a pattern requires a stringent adherence to the definition, as opposed to the majority of patterns that can be interpreted more loosely.

Wherever possible throughout this book I will be using the English name of the pattern, rather than the Japanese name. This will probably be simpler for you to remember, rather than struggling with a potential language barrier. Steve Nison, the author of _Japanese Candlestick Charting Techniques_, initially coined many of the Western names for candlestick patterns. He translated many original Japanese texts in order to release the secrets of the candle to Western society. Wherever possible, I will maintain consistency with the Nison translation and definition of the candlestick patterns displayed in this text. There are a few times where I must deviate, based on my own interpretation of a pattern. I will clearly identify those occasions to assist in consistency of terminology.

In my descriptions about the candlestick patterns, I refer to _periods_ or _sessions_. These terms are interchangeable and time-specific, meaning if you are looking at a daily chart, one session or period will refer to one day. On a weekly chart, a single trading session or period will represent one week. Even if I refer to a daily chart, the principles of the candlestick pattern discussed will still be relevant to all other time increments, e.g. weekly or monthly charts. The same principles behind the formation and the impact of the candle will hold true, regardless of the timeframe chosen. This is important to note in order to understand the implications of the next few sections of this book.

"A candlestick pattern will usually have an impact of between one and ten periods."

Candlesticks provide signals revealing the immediate emotional intensity of the traders involved with that instrument. However, it is wise to remember that there is a fine line between love and hate. A share that is adored by everyone may quickly be subject to selling pressure within a very short timeframe. For this reason the impact of the candlestick pattern is to be considered as short-term in nature. A candlestick pattern will usually have an impact of between one and ten periods.

The other important piece of terminology is the word candlestick _pattern_ or _formation_. Pattern and formation are interchangeable terms. A candlestick pattern may consist of one period, or several periods. I will explain this further as we explore the different patterns together.

Throughout this publication, in some of the charts depicted, I have chosen an ellipse or a circular shape to draw your attention to a candlestick. Other charts show a rectangle, or an arrow pointing to the particular pattern. There is no significance related to the shape that I have chosen. I merely chose the shape that visually blocks the least surrounding candles on the chart, in order for you to gain a clear view of all other candles shown.

Every form of trading involves an inherent level of risk. I am happy to share with you all that I have learned about this method, but understand that no single technique will provide correct signals every time. Unfortunately, there is no Holy Grail. I cannot promise that you will make money by simply reading this book. Trading excellence will take time and practice to develop. It is my goal to provide you with an insight about how to use this tool to enhance your own trading endeavours, but your own application of the techniques will determine your level of success.

CANDLES, LINE CHARTS AND BAR CHARTS

The three charts as shown in Fig. 1.1, Fig. 1.2 and Fig. 1.3 all represent the same information and the same time scale, however their graphical format ensures that each chart looks very different.

FIG. 1.1—NAB Daily Bar Chart

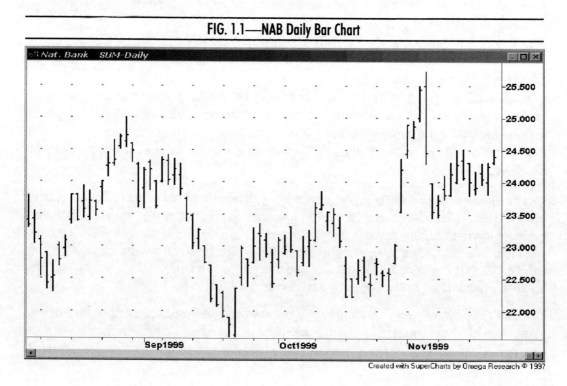

Created with SuperCharts by Omega Research ® 1997

FIG. 1.2—NAB Daily Line Chart

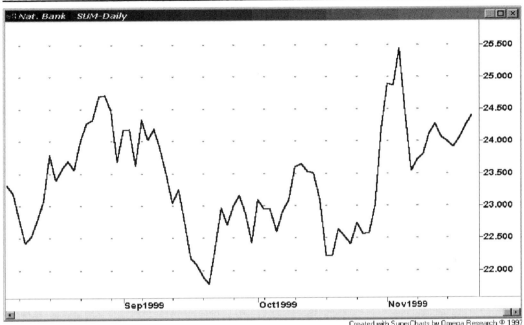

FIG. 1.3—NAB Daily Candlestick Chart

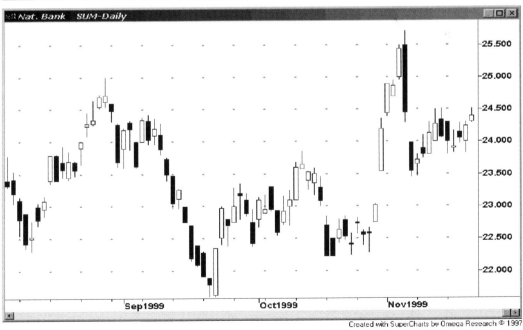

The individual building block of a bar chart is a single bar. Drawing a single bar requires an opening price, a high, a low and a closing price, (see Fig. 1.4). The vertical line shows the high and low of that period. The two horizontal lines depict the open and the close. The open is the horizontal line on the left of the vertical line, and the close is the horizontal line on the right of the vertical line.

FIG. 1.4—
A Single Western Bar

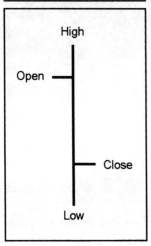

When many of these single-period bars are plotted on a chart with the time represented on the horizontal axis and the share price shown on the vertical axis, a traditional *bar chart* is created, (see Fig. 1.1).

A *line chart* connects the closing prices for each period, providing even less information, but it is perhaps a simpler chart to interpret in comparison to the bar chart, (see Fig. 1.2). This type of chart is usually provided in newspapers when a journalist depicts share price action.

A single-session candlestick represents the same data that you will find in a single bar, however it looks completely different. The origin of the name is obvious when looking at the chart. A *candlestick chart* looks like a series of candles with wicks, (see Fig. 1.3). (The wick, however, can be at either end of the candle.) Every part of the candle has specific implications.

The thick part of the candle is called the *real body*. This shows the range between the opening and the closing price, (see Fig. 1.5). The colour of the candle has very important implications. When the real body is white (or empty), it means that the close was higher than the opening price. When the real body is black (or filled in), it means that the close was lower than the opening price.

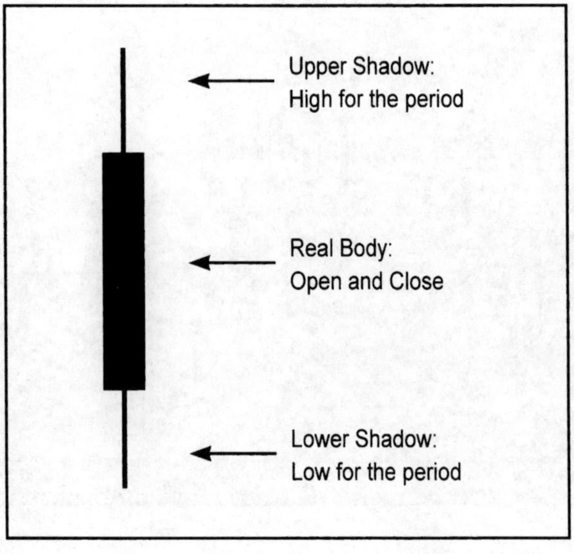

The thin lines above and below the real body of the candlestick are called the *wicks*, *shadows* or *tails* (regardless of on which side of the real body they are located). The upper shadow is the high for that

---

FIG. 1.5—A Candlestick

Upper Shadow:
High for the period

Real Body:
Open and Close

Lower Shadow:
Low for the period

period, and the lower shadow is the low for that period. The shadows are usually considered to be of less importance than the thick part of the candle, as they represent extraneous price fluctuations. They provide an indication about the extremes of emotion experienced by the bulls and the bears throughout that period.

OPEN AND CLOSE

The open and the close are the most emotionally-charged points of the day and therefore they are significant in candlestick analysis. There is a saying that "the amateurs open the market and the professionals close the market". The amateurs have had all night to absorb the rumours and news items about certain shares, and their anxious flurry of activity on the opening of the market reflects this. It is a well-known fact that in most markets around the world, the period of highest volatility for the day is the first hour of trading. This is definitely a feature of the Australian sharemarket. In the first hour of trading, there is a veritable scramble of punters trying to establish their positions. The more anxious the trader, the earlier he or she will place an order with a broker. Once this early-morning scramble calms down, the market settles into a less volatile period during the middle of the day.

The final hour of trading on the Australian sharemarket also experiences a definite increase in volatility as buyers and sellers review the price action that occurred during the day. They must quickly assess whether they can live with their trading decisions overnight, so they must be decisive and brave to buy or sell at the final hour. Emotions again run high as traders buy and sell their shares in accordance with their view of the direction of the market for the following day.

Traditionally the close of the day has been a critical component for many technical analysts in the options and futures markets. The closing prices establish the severity of margin calls for traders in options and futures, so many traders would prefer to close their positions rather than experience any negative consequences. (This explains why many traders utilise a line chart to analyse their shares as this type of chart places emphasis on the closing prices.)

If the professionals close the session at a higher price than the opening price (established by the amateurs), this has a powerful bullish impact. If the professionals close the market lower than the initial opening price, this has a bearish implication.

OTHER TIMEFRAMES

The same thought process also comes into play when viewing a weekly chart. A weekly chart shows the open as being the open on the first trading day for the week (usually a Monday) and the close as being the close on the last trading day for the week (usually a Friday). Many traders review their charts over the weekend and place their orders as soon as the market opens on a Monday. On a Friday, traders need to decide whether they can live with their open positions over the weekend, or whether to exit them. For this reason, candlestick charting is useful when using a weekly chart or a daily chart.

> "If the share is not especially volatile, or has low volume, an intra-day candlestick chart is unlikely to reveal any meaningful patterns."

Other timeframes are also appropriate when using candlestick charting, e.g. monthly charts or intra-day charts. I personally believe that candles are best used on intra-day charts, daily charts or weekly charts of volatile shares with reasonable volumes being traded. If the share is not especially volatile, or has low volume, an intra-day candlestick chart is unlikely to reveal any meaningful patterns. Monthly charts, while useful for overall trend definition, generally provide slower signals. They are mainly suitable for the longer-term investor (one year or greater).

THE WHITE CANDLE

The colour of the candle depicts whether it is bearish or bullish.

When a white candle is evident for a session, the bulls were in control and they managed to push the price to higher levels, (see Fig. 1.6). Some charting software packages use the colour green on screen to represent these bullish candles. In nature, green is the colour of growth (in plants, anyway), so it is easy to remember the meaning of a green candle.

Using colours in a candlestick chart is my personal preference. The colour assists in quick identification of candles that are very close together on a chart. When there are many candles present on a chart, sometimes it is difficult to distinguish which candles are white and which candles are black. (Examples throughout this book, however, will appear in white and black.)

FIG. 1.6—The White Candle

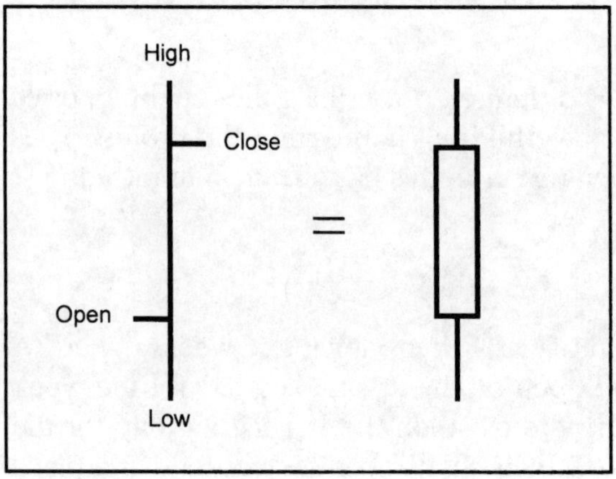

The basic psychology behind the white candle is that traders have decided, throughout the session, that they have a definite liking for this share. If the candle is *long*, and especially if it closes at its high for the session, it is as if the traders are all yelling in unison: "We adore this share. We like this share so much that we'd like to wallpaper our living room with buy certificates of this stock!"

When the day closes higher than it opened, it is a positive bullish sign in terms of market sentiment. There is demand for the share and buyers are willing to pay higher and higher prices. The price is driven up as demand outstrips supply. Greed compels people to purchase the share in the hope that prices will continue to be driven skyward.

Beanie Babies

To illustrate the point, here is a recent example of what happens when demand outstrips supply. The 'Beanie Babies' are a popular addition to the ever-expanding range of children's toys on the market. These cute little stuffed toys are collectable items which sometimes command up to $US350 per item! The manufacturers cleverly limit the supply of each series, in order to increase demand for individual versions of the toy. They also, from time to time, 'retire' (or discontinue) models by taking them off the market.

In the middle of 1999, a horror newsflash was broadcast on the Beanie Baby website, and in major newspapers such as _The Australian._ It announced that Ty Inc., the company responsible for bringing Beanie Babies into the world, would retire _all_ Beanies on 31 December 1999. To coincide with this announcement, they released a new Beanie Baby called 'The End' which was, ominously, black. Within minutes, chat rooms were packed with Beanie Baby lovers begging for answers. Prices at the online Beanie auction soared to record highs, and traffic at beanie.com tripled. The market was overwhelmed with buyers. Even my niece Melissa was overcome with Beanie fever. She suggested that I take the money that I have invested in shares and buy as many Beanie Babies as I could get my hands on!

This same psychology applies to the formation of a white candle. As is evident, when demand is greater than supply, the price will be driven upwards.

THE BLACK CANDLE

When the real body is black (or filled in), the close is lower than the opening price, (see Fig. 1.7). Some charting software packages use the colour red, instead of black. If you have ever been trapped in a losing trade, it can feel like your funds are 'bleeding'. The use of the colour red in this situation has similar connotations.

When the share closes lower than its opening price for the day, it is a sign that traders are liquidating their holdings.

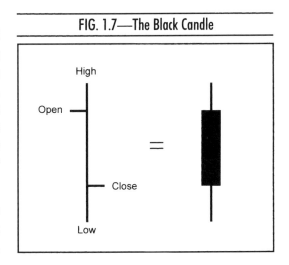

FIG. 1.7—The Black Candle

This has the effect of driving the share price down. The sellers have fear in their hearts and flood the market with their shares. Hence, the market sentiment is pessimistic, creating a far greater supply of shares. This causes the closing price to be lower than the opening price, and the result is the creation of a black candle.

If the share closes at its low for the day, the traders are in effect saying: "I have to dump this share at all costs! I totally dislike this share now and it is time to desert the sinking ship!" A black candle clearly shows that the bears were in control for that period.

WHEN TO USE CANDLESTICKS

Candlesticks are great for:

↪ identifying continuation patterns

↪ determining short-term trend direction changes, i.e. reversal patterns.

Continuation patterns suggest that the share will continue over the short term in a specific direction. Reversal patterns mean that the share will change direction completely, or simply flatten into a sideways trend, (see Fig. 1.8).

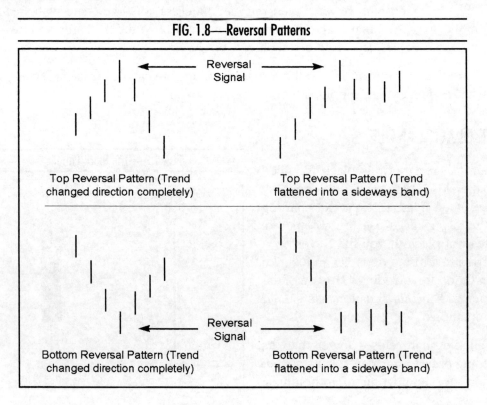

FIG. 1.8—Reversal Patterns

Reversal patterns are only predictive if they occur once the share is trending. If a share is already trading in a sideways band, then reversal patterns will not be effective. I have personally found reversal patterns to be an incredibly useful tool, so much of this book will be devoted to the recognition and use of these patterns. There are actually more examples of reversal candlestick signals than there are of continuation patterns.

The use of reversal patterns is generally related to entry and exit procedures. They often indicate that it is time to take profits on a position. Continuation patterns are more likely to be used to let you know whether to stay with a winning trade. They suggest that you should continue trading in the direction of the trend.

THE ELEMENTS OF THE CANDLE

Daniel Gramza, a US-based trader, is a worldwide authority on the use of candlesticks. Daniel has been a key mentor for many traders in this arena. His energy and enthusiasm for candlestick methods permeates his every statement. If you ever get the opportunity to see Daniel give a presentation, I highly recommend the experience!

He professes that there are several key elements to the formation of a candlestick. Let's review each element.

1) Candle Colour

As discussed, the colour of the candle is a major consideration in many candlestick patterns. White has bullish implications, and black indicates bearish selling pressure.

2) Candle Range

The range from the high to the low, or the peak of the upper shadow to the base of the lower shadow, is a general indicator of the level of volatility for that period.

3) Candle Body Size

The size of the real body can provide a clue as to the level of conviction of either the bulls or the bears. The presence of a long candle in relation to the most recent candles of previous days holds special significance. It is very likely that a _dominant candle_ will provide an indication as to immediate future trading activity. This dominant candle concept will be discussed more fully in Chapter 2 (p. 34).

A small bodied candle shows indecision by the bulls and the bears. Neither buyers nor sellers would appear to be unduly influencing the session characterised by a small real body.

When discussing candlestick patterns, the real body assumes a far greater significance than the candle range or the candle shadows. Most of the two- and three-line candle patterns (i.e. where more than one candlestick actually forms the pattern in its entirety) rely on a 'body-to-body' comparison. Although the candle range is important, it is actually the real body relationship to another candle's real body that is critical in defining patterns.

4) Shadow Location

The shadow provides an indication of buyer or seller strength. If there are long upper shadows at the top of an uptrend, this implies that the buyers have weakened and the sellers have begun to move in. If there are long lower shadows at the bottom of a downtrend, the price has dropped to a low enough level to encourage buyers to purchase the share. These *rejection patterns* are very easy to recognise.

5) Shadow Size

The length of the shadow complements the above discussion on shadow location. The longer the shadow, the greater the market rejection of the price levels being tested by that share. For example, long upper shadows suggest that the market cannot continue in the predominant uptrending direction for long. This is especially relevant if the share has displayed shadows in the past at that same price level.

6) Candle Development

By breaking down the time increment of a candle's *development*, an interesting story will often be revealed. For example, a black candle that represents one week may be made up of four bullish daily candles, and one decidedly bearish daily candle. Candle development dissects one candle to create many candles (of shorter time duration than the original).

Using the process of *candle addition* can assist in further ascertaining the ultimate meaning of a candlestick. This process adds the candles of several periods together to create just one candle. In effect, it takes the data from several periods and reduces it to one period.

Learning the processes of candle addition and candle development is similar to learning to transpose music, or becoming fluent in a language. Once you have developed sufficient skill in this area, you will be able to consistently perform these activities without undue effort.

Throughout the chapters on multiple candlestick patterns, I will provide many examples of candle addition. This will assist in revealing the true bullish or bearish implication of each formation, and hopefully develop your skill in this process.

7) Candle Location

It is necessary to examine several phases in order to understand the true meaning of a candlestick pattern. By disregarding one of these stages, the predictability regarding the outcome of a candlestick pattern will be limited.

There are three stages: the *lead-up*, the *trigger*, and the *confirmation* phase, (see Fig. 1.9).

The *lead-up* to the appearance of a candle pattern must be considered in order to assess the potential strength of the reversal or continuation pattern. The lead-up consists of the activity of several of the preceding candles. For example, reversal patterns are only relevant if the share has already been trending, and will not be as appropriate for use while a share has been range trading.

FIG. 1.9—The Lead-up, Trigger and Confirmation

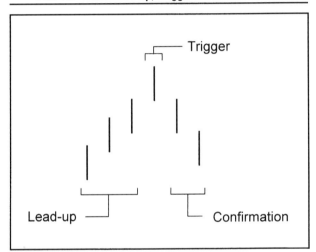

The *trigger* candle pattern is the actual appearance of a reversal or continuation pattern. For a one-line candle, the trigger will be represented by one session only. For more complex two-line patterns, the trigger will include two sessions, etc. (Note that I may refer to a multiple-line candlestick pattern in its entirety as a 'candle', rather than separating each of its components. This terminology is widely considered to be appropriate.)

Inexperienced traders who learn about the power of the candle are most likely to place all of their emphasis on the appearance of the trigger. If you look only at the trigger, and ignore the lead-up and confirmation phase, you will not receive the full benefit of utilising candles to their maximum potential. Every phase is of equal importance.

Confirmation regarding the effectiveness of the candlestick is also an essential component of using this method of analysis. Some candlestick patterns require greater levels of confirmation than others. We will discuss which patterns require heightened levels of confirmation, and the strength of specific candles, as we progress through each of the patterns in subsequent chapters.

This micro-study of a candlestick pattern must also be viewed in the context of the overall market environment. For example, if a share is in a mature stage in comparison to a newly-introduced share, this will have a marked effect on the interpretation of a candlestick. Previous levels of support and resistance must also be considered.

CHAPTER REVIEWS

At the end of key chapters I have provided a section for you to complete to test your knowledge. The study of candlesticks is quite detailed, so by taking the time to review each section before progressing, your retention will be greatly assisted. See how you go with this first one.

REVIEW

1) Reversal patterns could mean that the trend is flattening *or* changing direction (circle the correct answer):

(a) True   (b) False   ✓

2) The real body of a candlestick represents (circle the correct answer):

(a) The closing price and the high for that session.

(b) The opening price and the closing price.   ✓

(c) The high and the low.

– read notes! ✓

3) Name the seven main elements of a candlestick:

Colour, range, body size, shadow location, size, candle development, location

4) Figure 1.10 shows three standard bars from a bar chart. Convert these bar charts to candlesticks by drawing your answers in the spaces provided.

FIG. 1.10—Bar to Candle Conversions

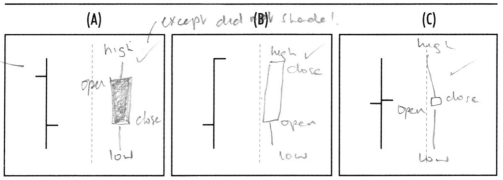

(A)   *except did r(B) shade!*   *(C)*

5) In general, is a white candle bullish or bearish? Why?

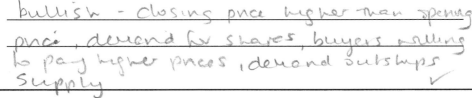

bullish – closing price higher than opening price, demand for shares, buyers willing to pay higher prices, demand outstrips supply ✓

(left margin, rotated) open always on left, close on right

ANSWERS

1) True. A reversal pattern means that there is a *change* in the direction of the trend. This could mean a flattening of the trend. Alternatively, it could also mean a swing from an uptrend to a downtrend, or from a downtrend to an uptrend.

2) (b) is the correct answer. The opening and closing prices represent the real body for that period. These are the most emotionally-charged points of the session.

3) The seven elements of a candlestick are: candle colour, candle range, candle body size, shadow location, shadow size, candle development and candle location.

4) See Fig. 1.11 for the answers.

FIG. 1.11—Bar to Candle Conversions

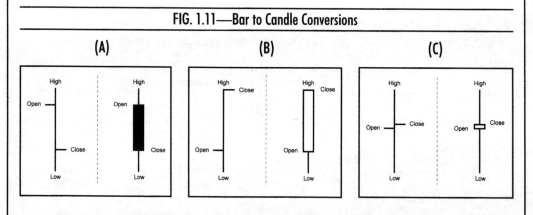

5) A white candle is bullish as it closed higher than it opened for that session. Demand outstripped supply, so prices were driven upwards.

➔ ➔ ➔ *Now that you have conquered some of the basic concepts, let's have a look at some single-line candlestick reversal patterns...* ➔ ➔ ➔

Chapter 2

SINGLE-LINE CANDLE REVERSAL PATTERNS

The topic for this chapter is a reversal in trend brought about by the appearance of a single candlestick. These patterns are the simplest to memorise and interpret. They are sometimes called *one-line* or *single-line reversals*. They often have an incredibly powerful impact. Subsequent chapters will build on the complexity of these patterns, so take the time to understand each signal before reading on. You may need to refer back to this chapter to remember the names of some of these basic one-line candles. I have also included a list of each pattern in the Candlesticks Table of Contents on pages iii and iv. This may act as a quick reference guide, as well as directing you to the appropriate page when you require a refresher on a particular candlestick pattern.

As you will remember, reversal patterns suggest that after a share has been trending for some time, a change in direction of the trend could be imminent. Either the share price will change direction completely, or it may simply flatten into a sideways trading band, (see Fig. 1.8, page 14).

The small bars before and after the candlestick formation in the coming examples show the direction of the preceding and following prices on the chart. They have no other special significance in these examples. They are placed on the diagram to assist your understanding of the reversal implications of the candlestick pattern.

For each example of a candlestick pattern, I will show you the ideal *lead-up* situation, the actual *trigger* pattern, and then suggest the level of *confirmation* required. The possible *psychological principles* that have caused this type of pattern to develop will also be discussed. Where necessary, an example of this pattern in an actual share chart will be provided. For multiple-line candlestick patterns, I will also give you an example of how this formation reduces to a one-line candle via the process of candle addition. This format will remain consistent throughout any discussion of candlestick patterns in this book.

It is important to note that whenever gaps or *windows* (as they are known in candlestick terminology) are present before and after the trigger candle, the strength of that candlestick pattern intensifies. This is especially relevant in relation to one-line candlestick patterns. Gaps show that the price activity of the new candlestick is completely above or below the preceding period. When accompanied by significant volume, gaps can display powerful shifts in market sentiment.

A WORD ON CONFIRMATION...

It is wise to await confirmation regarding the effectiveness of the candle prior to taking any action. Just how much confirmation is necessary? Here are some guidelines.

There are several methods that you can use to ascertain whether a pattern is confirmed. One method is to check on the market activity of the session following a bearish trigger candle at 3.30 p.m., just prior to the close for the day. This may provide confirmation to exit long positions and/or enter short positions. This method may help avoid a less graceful exit of a long position if the share gaps down to a lower price at the opening of the following session.

Other traders may choose to exit long positions at the opening price of the confirmation candle that appears immediately after a bearish trigger candle. This may provide a number of false signals, as the market could trend contrary to your expectations during that session.

Another alternative is to wait for a complete session or two after the trigger candle to confirm the new market direction. This will conservatively provide the least number of false signals; however, the new market trend may have already been established, so your entry or exit may not be as close to the actual turning point as it could have been.

Consider the term of your view. Medium-term investors are likely to require a greater level of confirmation in comparison to shorter-term traders. For the purposes of clarity, I will define a short-term trader as having a view that spans one hour to three months. A medium-term trader can be assumed to have a six- to nine-month view, and a long-term trader is interested in investments which are expected to provide a return in one year or more. (Obviously the distinctions between the duration of each term are somewhat subjective. These terms are expressed only to provide a guideline.)

In relation to the confirmation phase, if there has been a frequently occurring pattern with very predictable results, more aggressive traders could act on the basis of the trigger candle alone. For example, BHP is very responsive to a candlestick formation—that, you will find, is our agenda in Chapter 3—called an *engulfing pattern*. With this in mind, if you believe you have anticipated the completion of this trigger pattern, you could make an appropriate entry or exit prior to the market closing. Attentive traders with a short-term perspective find this technique very profitable.

The issue of the amount of confirmation required after the appearance of a trigger candle is a personal decision. More aggressive, short-term traders may choose to take hasty action after the appearance of a trigger candle. Conservative players with a medium- or long-term view are more likely to seek greater levels of confirmation.

Let's have a closer look at some single-line reversal patterns.

THE SHOOTING STAR

Description

This top reversal pattern displays an upper shadow length that is at least two times the length of the real body, (see Fig. 2.1). There is typically no lower shadow, or a very small lower shadow.

This pattern belongs to the family of *stars* which are characterised by small real bodies with gaps above or below a previous session's long body. Stars form a part of many candle reversal patterns and indicate market indecision.

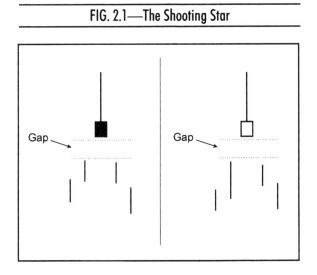

FIG. 2.1—The Shooting Star

Star bottom reversal patterns are sometimes referred to as *raindrops*. The presumed origin of the name raindrop is that the downpour of rain (or bearish activity in this situation) looks like it is easing. Raindrops have formed instead of the torrential storm that was apparent at an earlier stage.

The colour of the shooting star can be either white or black, however a black candle increases the bearish implications of the shooting star. Note that this principle of colour variation holds true for all *single* candlestick patterns, as well as for all *star* patterns. Either colour is appropriate, however black candles will increase the intensity of a bearish signal. White candles are not considered as bearish even if they form the same trigger candle. For example, a black top reversal pattern is more bearish than a white top reversal pattern.

The opposite holds true for any one-line bullish candlestick reversal patterns. A white bullish bottom reversal pattern is likely to have a greater impact than a black bullish bottom reversal pattern.

Candle Location

The lead-up to the shooting star candle is that the underlying instrument must be in an uptrend prior to the appearance of this trigger. (If you would like a refresher on the definition of an uptrend, or support and resistance, perhaps skip forward and read the first few paragraphs of Chapter 7, and then return to this discussion on specific candlesticks.)

For this pattern to fulfil the strictest definition there must be a gap present between the previous candle and the shooting star, as well as after the appearance of the trigger candle. I have found that even if a gap is not present, the shooting star represents a powerful reversal signal.

The confirmation required to complete this candlestick pattern is that the upper shadow and the real body of the candle following the trigger must be completely underneath the entire trading range of the shooting star. The appearance of this gap after the shooting star adds strength to the signal. A less stringent confirmation would ensure that the real body of the candle following the trigger was underneath the real body of the shooting star, but the shadows of the confirmation candle would be permitted to overlap with the trigger.

Whether you decide that the trigger candle is confirmed just before the closing session of the next period or after the close of the next period is up to you. As discussed, your level of aggression, and the term of your view, makes the level of confirmation required a personal choice.

Psychology

In the lead-up phase, the market has been in uptrend. The bulls have established dominance. Traders have been reluctant to sell to date, and have been more likely to add to their long positions. (A long position assumes a bullish perspective, and a short position assumes a bearish perspective.)

At the beginning of the period that forms the trigger candle, it seems that this bullish sentiment will continue. There is usually a gap from the previous candle, and the price begins to rise in relation to its opening value. However, at some time throughout the day, sellers decide to take profits. This creates a situation of rejection of higher price levels as the bulls are unable to continue driving share prices upwards. The rally of that period cannot be sustained.

In relation to the creation of the trigger candle, if the market closes at a lower level than its opening price, this is an even stronger sign of seller pressure. This will result in the formation of a black shooting star.

Whether white or black, this is an example of a bearish *rejection pattern* due to the long upper shadow visible in the shooting star formation.

If the market continues to trade at lower levels after the appearance of this trigger candle, it is likely that the uptrend has been reversed. When the shooting star hits, run for cover!

Example

Figure 2.2 shows the halt of three separate uptrends in NAB. A shooting star signified the uptrend reversal in each case. The sellers moved in and took profits, which resulted in a shift in market sentiment to a bearish perspective. The long tails show clear rejection of higher prices as the bulls failed to continue the price rally throughout each trigger candle session. Often a share will show a predisposition towards a candlestick formation. From this chart, it seems that NAB favours the shooting star to signify a reversal of uptrend.

FIG. 2.2—NAB Daily Chart Shooting Star

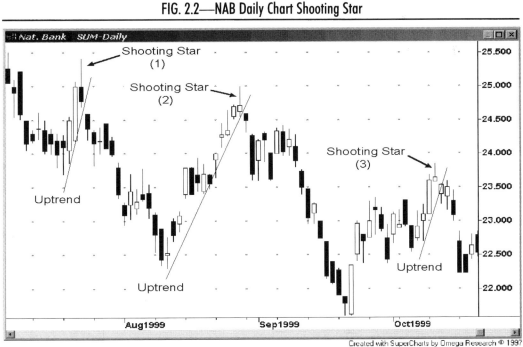

Created with SuperCharts by Omega Research ® 1997

Notice with the shooting stars (1) and (2), a small lower tail is present. In addition, gaps before and after the trigger candles would have been ideal, but are not evident on this chart. These slight variations from the exact definition of this pattern are examples of the latitude that traders must allow for candlestick analysis.

Some analysts prefer to call a shooting star without the presence of gaps an *inverted hanging man*. Regardless of how you decide to define this pattern, there can be no doubt that its implication is bearish.

The next candlestick that we will review is the hammer. This is a mirror image of a shooting star and it can signal the reversal of a downtrend.

THE HAMMER

Description

This bottom reversal pattern displays a lower shadow length that is at least two times the length of the real body. There is typically no upper shadow, or a very small upper shadow.

As you can see, this is the inverse of a shooting star, (see Fig. 2.3). It always appears as a bottom trend reversal, rather than at the top of a trend. The translation of the Japanese name for this pattern is 'trying to gauge the depth of the water by feeling for the bottom'. The other concept behind this name is that the market is trying to hammer out a base before progressing to new higher prices. As you can see, the shape resembles an actual hammer, which makes this a very easy pattern to remember.

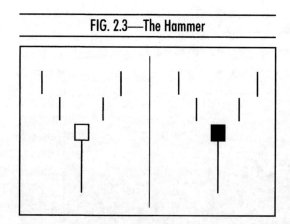

FIG. 2.3—The Hammer

The hammer clearly depicts the premise that the price has become low enough for buyers to enter the market with gusto. Although either colour is acceptable, a white candle will increase the bullish significance of this candle.

Candle Location

The lead-up to the hammer is that the share must be in a downtrend prior to the trigger candle. Gaps between each candle would be ideal, but are not strictly necessary.

The confirmation is either a gap up from the trigger candle, which involves the entire range of the subsequent candle, or just from the real body. Obviously, the greater the gap, the greater the bullish significance. Any trading activity above the real body of the hammer would be a bullish sign.

Psychology

In the lead-up phase, the market has been in downtrend. The bears have established dominance. If they have been dealing with this share at all in recent times, traders have been 'shorting', rather than buying the actual share.

There are approximately 250 shares that can be short-sold on the Australian market. The premise behind this activity is that traders sell shares to initiate the transaction, and then to buy them back at a later date, at a cheaper price. Traders who short-sell are expecting a share price decrease in order to make a profit. Writing a call option, or buying a put option or warrant, is another way to benefit from a downtrending share. Although I will not be going into detail about these strategies in this book, it is important to note that there are ways to make money when the market is trending downwards.

At the beginning of the period that forms the trigger candle, it seems that this bearish sentiment will continue. However, at some time throughout the session, buyers have moved in, and traders who have shorted the market have hastily covered their positions by buying the share. Strength is added to the trigger candle.

This scenario creates a situation of rejection of lower price levels. The rejection is clearly evident because of the long lower shadow. If this shadow also touched a previous level of support, this increases the power of the hammer. The downward thrust of that period cannot be sustained. It is important to note that a white hammer would have more bullish implications than a black hammer.

If the market continues to trade at higher levels after the appearance of this trigger candle, it is likely that the downtrend has been reversed, at least in the short term. I consider it to be of bullish significance if the hammer occurred on low volume levels, and the confirmation shows a volume increase. This reinforces the strength of the pattern.

A related formation to the hammer is the inverted hammer. This is the next pattern to be discussed.

THE INVERTED HAMMER

Description

This bottom reversal pattern displays a long upper shadow length that is at least two times the length of the real body. There is typically no lower shadow, or a very small lower shadow, in this formation.

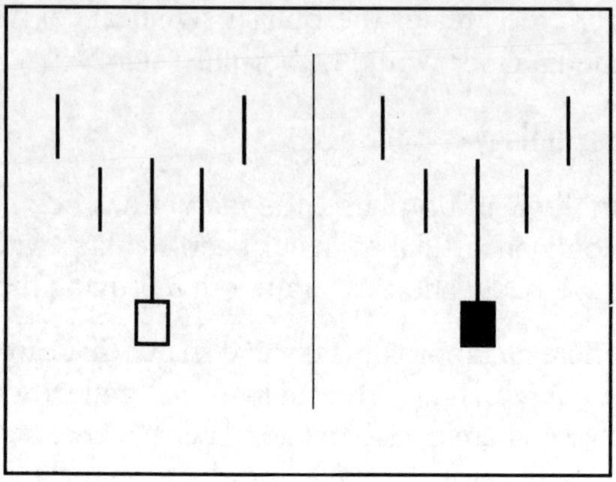

The inverted hammer is similar to the hammer, but it appears upside-down on a candlestick chart, (see Fig. 2.4). As with the hammer, this inverted version will often lead to a downtrend reversal. In relation to the candle location, everything that you have learned about the hammer is also relevant for this pattern.

Psychology

In the lead-up phase, the market has been in downtrend. The bears have established dominance. When the inverted hammer forms, the market 'tests' prices at a higher level. The price is driven up substantially throughout the course of the period that forms the trigger, but the bulls fall back by the close of this session. (For this reason, the hammer represents a stronger, more definite signal than the inverted hammer. The clear sign of rejection of lower prices is evident with the long lower tail of the hammer.) During the formation of the inverted hammer the bulls tried on those new higher prices for size, but a distinctive rally did not occur, otherwise a long white candle would have formed. A long white candle would have had a greater bullish inference.

In order to detect any false bullish signals, confirmation should be more vigorous in comparison to levels required for a hammer. Wait for a gap, or another sign of significant bullish behaviour, before acting on an inverted hammer signal.

In general, it is easier for a market to lose confidence than for a market to gain confidence. For this reason, any ambiguous bottom reversal patterns will require greater levels of confirmation prior to acting. It is important, however, also to pay attention to any top reversal patterns, even if they do not fulfil the exact definition. Markets often increase in value slowly, but experience bouts of fast and panicky declines, so the importance of a top reversal assumes special significance. The bulls tediously climb the mountain, whilst the bears happily abseil down it. The bears can move in with a speed that can take a trader's breath away! Downward corrections and the occasional sharemarket crash provide evidence that the speed of a decline is usually greater than the speed of an increase in market value.

FIG. 2.4—The Inverted Hammer

THE HANGING MAN

Description

This forbidding top reversal displays a long lower shadow length that is at least two times the length of the real body, (see Fig. 2.5). There is typically no upper shadow, or a very small upper shadow. It is easy to see how this pattern derived its name. It resembles an actual hanging man (i.e. the real body), complete with dangling legs (i.e. the lower shadow).

The hanging man is similar to the shooting star, but upside-down. Like the shooting star, it reverses an uptrend. In relation to the candle location, everything that you have learned about the shooting star is also relevant for this pattern.

FIG. 2.5—The Hanging Man

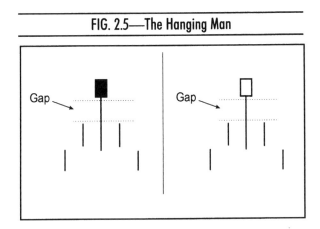

Because the hanging man does not display the violent level of rejection of higher prices as shown by the upper shadow of the shooting star, it would sound logical to believe that it is not a strong signal. If you remember, however, that markets lose confidence quickly, you will realise that the hanging man is a very potent signal. Do not make the mistake of ignoring it.

A shooting star and a hanging man are likely to reverse uptrends, while the hammer and inverted hammer patterns may reverse a downtrend.

Psychology

In the lead-up phase, the market has been in uptrend. The hanging man tested some lower prices, which has shaken the confidence of the bulls. Faith in the instrument has diminished, leaving the share vulnerable to bearish pressure. For a share to continue a sustained rally, investor confidence is essential. If confidence is shaken in any way, a decline in prices is likely to occur. Traders who are in profit may be vulnerable to selling pressure. This could create a chain reaction of fear as more and more sellers decide to offer their wares.

THE DOJI

Description

The doji describes any single-line candle that has approximately the same opening and closing prices, (see Fig. 2.6). The real body must be negligible in size, so even if the open and close are very close together, it will still be called a doji.

Due to the visual appearance of the doji, it is sometimes called a *doji cross*, especially when it is combined with other candlesticks, e.g. a *harami cross*. A doji serves as a top reversal pattern, as well as a bottom reversal pattern.

FIG. 2.6—The Doji

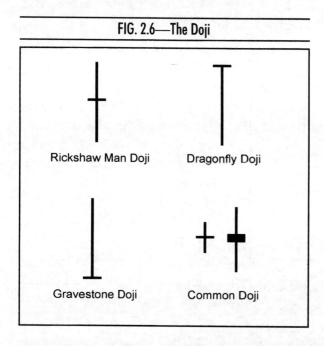

Rickshaw Man Doji   Dragonfly Doji

Gravestone Doji   Common Doji

There are several types of doji. Each has the same impact, regardless of whether they are defined as a *rickshaw man*, a *dragonfly*, a *gravestone* or a *common doji*.

The name doji was originally derived from the Japanese word for 'feudal lord'. These fearsome warriors were not exactly the types of guys that you would happily bring home to meet your mother, unless you had some serious issues with your family! They were very fond of chopping off people's heads if they believed they were not being shown the proper amount of respect. It seems that the primary goal in life of these feudal lords was the acquisition of neighbouring territories, and the total destruction of anyone who dared to stand in their way.

Feudal lords tended to prefer to make hill-like areas their control base, rather than deciding to live in the valleys. They also preferred for their domination to be so complete that no other rival feudal lord would be found within a significant radius. These principles assist in explaining why a doji at the top of a trend (on top of a hill) is more powerful than a bottom reversal doji (in a valley). If there are many doji present in the chart, the significance of each doji is markedly diminished. (Note: The plural of doji is simply 'doji'.)

One of the reasons why the Japanese language encourages some 'vague' statements is because, in many ways, it is safer to be vague, and err on the side of caution, rather than risk offending. This practice is likely to have saved many heads from rolling in the past. In relation to candlestick charting, however, this vagueness has led to some non-specific directions regarding the appropriate definition of patterns or the suggested level of confirmation required. For this reason, I have largely created my own levels of confirmation, based on my experience with candlestick charting.

Candle Location

The lead-up to the doji is that the share must be trending prior to the trigger candle. If a doji appears, often the share will reverse its upward direction and begin to downtrend, and vice versa. Gaps between the lead-up and the trigger candle would be ideal, but are not strictly necessary. If the doji is successful in reversing the trend, the result will be immediate.

The confirmation is preferably a counter-trend gap away from the trigger candle, which involves the entire range of the subsequent candle. Obviously, the greater the gap, the greater the significance. Any counter-trend move after the appearance of a doji implies confirmation.

Psychology

The reason for the awesome strength of the doji is the psychological importance of its message. A doji suggests a *balance* of demand and supply. Whenever the buyers and sellers agree on a price, a trend in the market will cease to exist. Trends by their very definition demand that either the bulls or the bears establish dominance, so the doji signifies the end of one trend and the beginning of a new trend. As a minimum, it suggests a significant pause in market activity, prior to the continuation of the overall trend. It is probably the most powerful candle available due to the lessons about trader behaviour that it confers.

Figures 2.7 and 2.8 (overleaf) display the power of some of the candles that we have learned about so far.

FIG. 2.7—BHP Daily

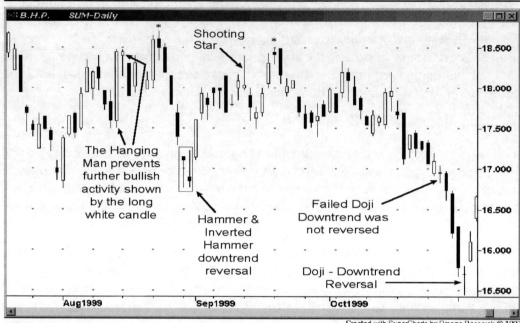

Shooting Star

The Hanging Man prevents further bullish activity shown by the long white candle

Hammer & Inverted Hammer downtrend reversal

Failed Doji Downtrend was not reversed

Doji - Downtrend Reversal

Aug1999   Sep1999   Oct1999

Created with SuperCharts by Omega Research © 1997

FIG. 2.8—BHP Daily

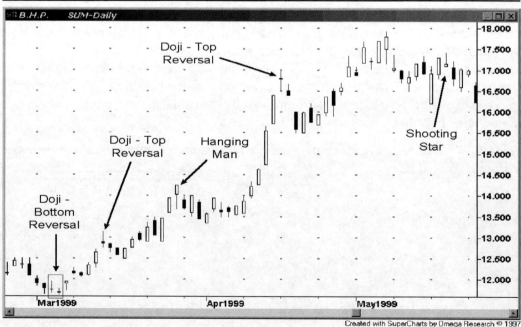

Doji - Top Reversal

Doji - Top Reversal

Hanging Man

Doji - Bottom Reversal

Shooting Star

Mar1999   Apr1999   May1999

Created with SuperCharts by Omega Research © 1997

THE SPINNING TOP

Description

This pattern is very similar to the doji, but there is a greater range from the opening to the closing price which forms a slightly thicker body. This greater range ensures that the spinning top is not quite as powerful as the doji, but it is still an incredibly important signal. It is easy to see how this candle derived its name, as it looks similar to the toy tops that many of us used to play with as children.

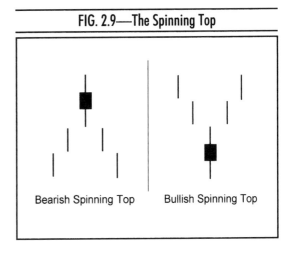

FIG. 2.9—The Spinning Top

Bearish Spinning Top   Bullish Spinning Top

The tail length is largely unimportant, and the candle can be either white or black. It represents a tug of war between the bulls and the bears and is accentuated by the presence of a gap before and after the trigger candle (see Fig. 2.9). As with the doji, the spinning top can reverse either an uptrend or a downtrend. Look back at Fig. 2.7 to see if you can spot a couple of spinning tops within the first half of the chart. I have marked these with an asterisk to assist in your recognition.

The principles regarding candle location and the psychology of the doji are applicable to the spinning top.

OTHER TYPES OF CANDLES

There are several other types of candles which do not signify a reversal or continuation, but are necessary to define, as they form the basis for many other patterns. These are listed below.

THE MARUBOZU OR SHAVEN CANDLE

Description

These long candles have no shadows on either end, (see Fig 2.10). For a bullish candle, this is considered to be extremely strong, yet in a somewhat contradictory fashion, the black bearish version is often claimed to indicate that the downtrend may be running out of puff.

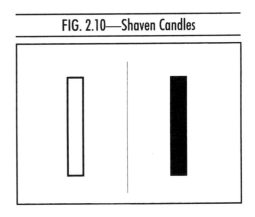

FIG. 2.10—Shaven Candles

Personally, I have found that the first appearance of a shaven candle after a share has been trading in a defined range is incredibly significant. It is my view that if a share breaks out of a trading band with a shaven candle, on heavy volume, this is a powerful indication that the direction of the move initiated by the candle is likely to continue within subsequent trading periods.

THE SHORT CANDLE

Description

These candles have a short real body with small or negligible shadows, (see Fig. 2.11). Typically these candles personify indecision. They may indicate confusion about whether the bulls or bears are in control, or perhaps that the speculators are biding their time prior to an announcement. The ultimate short candle is the doji.

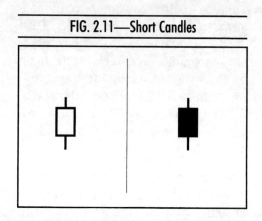

FIG. 2.11—Short Candles

After a strong move, it is common to see a short day, as the market pauses to catch its breath before continuing with its vigorous trending activity. Neither the bulls nor the bears have a dominating upper hand during this trading session.

THE LONG AND DOMINANT CANDLE

Description

Both a *long* and a *dominant* candle have a long real body. They often, but not necessarily, have small or negligible shadows.

I consider a candle to be *dominant* if it is significantly larger in length in relation to the other candles within the chart, especially within the most recent trading sessions. To fulfil my definition of dominant, this candle must be accompanied by *high relative volume*. Notice the increase in volume in comparison to the earlier sessions at the appearance of the dominant candle in Powertel, (see Fig. 2.12).

In my view, a candle may be termed as *long* even if there are several other long candles in the preceding periods. Volume is not a key indicator when describing a *long* candle, whereas it is an essential component in the creation of a *dominant* candle. For this reason, the terms of long and dominant are *not* interchangeable. A dominant candle has a much greater impact than a long candle. A dominant candle indicates a violent unequivocal decision about the future market direction. The dominant candle clearly shows the victory of either the bulls (white candle) or the bears (black candle).

FIG. 2.12—Powertel Daily and the Dominant Candle

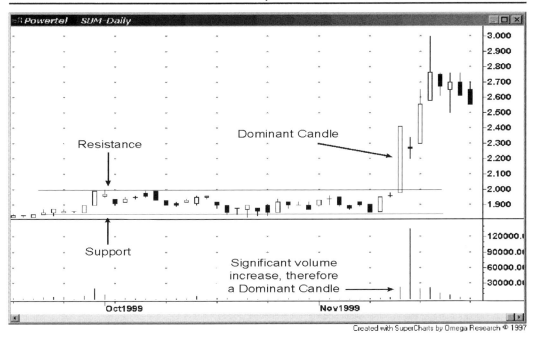

FIG. 2.13—Wattyl Daily and the Long Candle

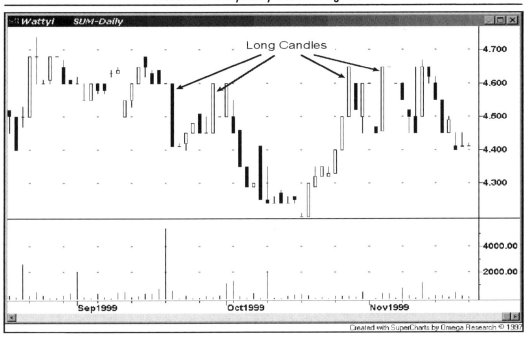

As you can see in Fig. 2.13, there are many long candles in the Wattyl chart, but they do not have a lasting impact on the share price direction. If there are many long candles apparent in a chart, the only way to detect a dominant candle is by a dramatic increase in volume after the share has made a clean break above or below a support/resistance line.

Some analysts refer to these dominant candles as the *benchmark candle*. Other analysts do not distinguish between dominant/benchmark candles and long candles. I believe that the distinction between these two types of candles is essential.

This concept of the dominant candle is of key importance in my trading strategy. It assists in the determination of support/resistance levels, helps to establish profit targets, and can facilitate the identification of sustainable breakouts. I will discuss these concepts in more detail throughout later chapters. For now though, be aware that I am exceptionally attentive whenever I notice the appearance of a dominant candle.

REJECTION PATTERNS

Having looked at these reversal patterns and some other important candles, it is now useful to consider two rejection patterns.

BEARISH REJECTION

Description

This pattern is evident when several shaven real bodies and/or highs for an instrument experience resistance at approximately the same price level. This is a bearish form of rejection, (see Fig. 2.14). The buyers are rejecting higher prices, and the sellers' efforts to sell at higher levels are ignored. The buying demand at higher prices has dried up.

The ideal form of bearish rejection, in my view, is where several upper shadows are evident at approximately the same price at the top of a trend. These long upper shadows are my key to recognising that the share is

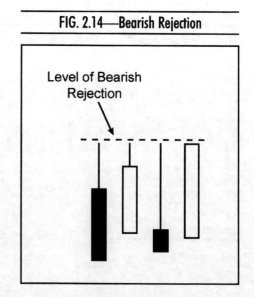

FIG. 2.14—Bearish Rejection

Level of Bearish Rejection

having difficulty closing above this price level. This has a bearish implication as selling activity undermines the power of any bullish uptrend.

Even if it takes you a while to understand the implications of many of the candlesticks in this book, try to cement the concept of 'rejection' in your mind. The principle behind this idea forms the basis for many top reversals, such as the shooting star. It is a key indication that I seek to observe selling pressure and the possible reversal of an uptrend.

BULLISH REJECTION

Description

A bullish form of rejection occurs when several shaven real bodies and/or lows for an instrument experience support at approximately the same price level, (see Fig. 2.15). The buyers have begun to dictate their preferred price level to purchase the share. Sellers are not prepared to sell at less than these prices. Selling pressure evident in the downtrend has converted to buying pressure. The prices of the shares have become low enough to encourage buyers to enter the market.

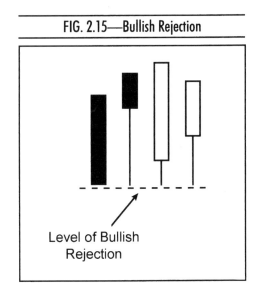

FIG. 2.15—Bullish Rejection

Level of Bullish Rejection

The ideal bottom reversal rejection pattern, in my view, is where several lower shadows are evident at approximately the same price at the bottom of a trend. These long lower shadows are my key to recognising that the share is having difficulty closing below this price level. This has a bullish implication as buying activity has been occurring at this same price level. It is as if the market is in agreement that the share price is a bargain at this level. A bullish trend is likely to ensue after the appearance of several of these long lower shadows.

Although these signs of rejection are not recognised as a standard, traditional candlestick, I have found this concept to be invaluable in my own trading. Very clear support and resistance lines are often formed due to these patterns.

I have observed that the candle tends to provide several signals that are outside the realms of traditional analysis. I would like to provide these for you so that you can benefit from my observations and use them to trade the market productively.

REVIEW

1) A doji is a more powerful signal than a spinning top:

   (a) True   (b) False

2) A hammer and an inverted hammer have bullish implications and occur at the bottom of a trend:

   (a) True   (b) False

3) Single-line candlesticks represent very strong signals. They do not require confirmation at all:

   (a) True   (b) False

4) A dominant candle is a long day of either colour with high volume. They are of even more significance if they penetrate a previously-established support/resistance level:

   (a) True   (b) False

5) Look at Fig. 2.16. Circle and name any candlestick formations that you recognise.

FIG. 2.16—CBA Daily

Created with SuperCharts by Omega Research ® 1997

ANSWERS

1) (a) True. Any pattern with a very small real body represents a market in a state of balance. There is indecision on the part of the bulls and the bears regarding who is winning the tug of war. For this reason, a doji represents this indecision to a greater degree than a spinning top.

2) (a) True. A hammer and an inverted hammer have bullish implications. They are bottom reversals and can often indicate the reversal of a downtrend.

3) (b) False. Even though candlesticks are remarkable analytical tools, they require confirmation prior to acting in order to establish their effectiveness. Even the best analytical tool presents false signals from time to time. Stack the odds of a successful trade in your favour by waiting until the signal is confirmed. Trading is, to a large degree, about discovering tools that will increase the probability of entering a profitable trade. Candles represent another tool to add to the weight of evidence of other indicators to increase your probability of entering successful trades.

4) (a) True. A dominant candle is a powerful indication of market sentiment. It is a long candle with significant volume relative to the previous trading sessions. If a white dominant candle breaks through a well-established resistance line, the effect is undeniably bullish. If a black dominant candle breaks through a well-established support line, a bearish trend is likely to begin.

5) See Fig. 2.17 (overleaf) for suggested answers. Be aware that there are many other candlestick patterns present on this chart. I have provided you with the major formations only.

FIG. 2.17—CBA Daily

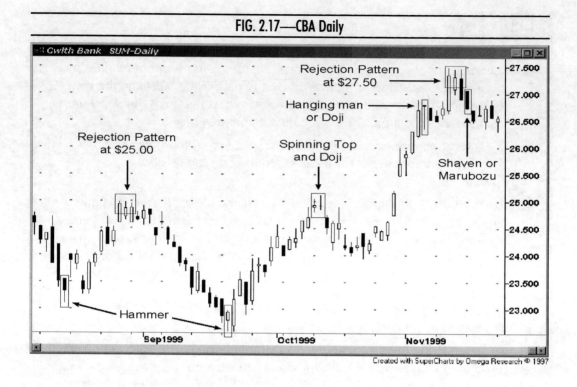

Cwlth Bank SUM-Daily

Rejection Pattern
at $27.50

Hanging man
or Doji

Rejection Pattern
at $25.00

Spinning Top
and Doji

Shaven or
Marubozu

Hammer

Sep1999   Oct1999   Nov1999

Created with SuperCharts by Omega Research ® 1997

➜   ➜   ➜   *There are many candlestick patterns composed of the trading activity of greater than one period. The next chapter will reveal the most valuable of the two-line candle reversals...* ➜   ➜   ➜

Chapter 3

TWO-LINE CANDLE

REVERSAL PATTERNS

Some candlestick patterns are composed of two or more candles which, when viewed together, have either a bullish or a bearish interpretation.

To fully understand whether these signals are likely to have a positive or negative effect on the share price, it helps to combine the separate candles that make up the multiple-line formation. In essence, this is a method of taking the candles of two or more periods and reducing the time scale to one period. This results in a single candle being drawn, instead of the original number of candles. This is the process of *candle addition*. I believe that Daniel Gramza coined this phrase. Other analysts such as Gregory Morris have called this process *candle breakdown.*

For example, five individual daily candles may form a weekly doji. This single weekly candle takes the open for the first day, the close for the last day, the overall high for the week and the overall low for the week. Using this data, a single candle can be drawn, rather than five separate candles. The process of candle addition takes each of those five sessions and creates one candle.

Using this same example, *candle development* would take the single doji and work backwards to separate each day's trading activity into five individual candles. Candle development separates trading sessions and candle addition combines trading sessions. Each process provides a greater depth of understanding about the nature of a specific candlestick.

"Candle development separates trading sessions and candle addition combines trading sessions."

The process of candle development, as well as candle addition, is important to understand. This knowledge will greatly assist your ability to decide whether the predominant implication of a pattern is bullish or bearish.

For each of the two- and three-line candles that we will discuss, I will use the process of candle addition to ascertain the level of confirmation required, and whether the meaning of the formation is unambiguously bullish or bearish. This process will complement your view about the direction in which a share is likely to trend. This is a major reason why a full understanding of single-line candles is essential.

BACK-TESTING

It is interesting to note that some shares repeatedly favour the same candlestick pattern. As you will remember, in Fig. 2.2 on page 25 we saw that NAB consistently favoured the shooting star for reversal of an uptrend. This type of market knowledge will assist you greatly in your trading. When you have identified a share that displays a candlestick reversal or continuation pattern, it is prudent to delve into history to see whether the share has been responsive to that type of formation in the past. This type of back-testing is very useful and will increase your probability of successful trades based on candlesticks.

Getting to know the shares you are trading will greatly assist you in your efforts to understand which patterns will provide the biggest impact. It is almost as if each share has developed its own personality that predisposes it towards being exceptionally reactive to some formations.

THE THREE-POINT BACK-TESTING PLAN

Whilst reviewing the chart history of the share, I have found that it is helpful to note three main aspects. Look for:

➥ The *frequency* of pattern occurrence.

➥ The *immediate responsiveness* to individual patterns.

➥ The longer-term *effectiveness* of these formations.

For example, if there are many doji on a chart (the *frequency*) that did not appear to influence the share price action, then the appearance of a new doji is likely to be ineffective. The appearance of an infrequent, but powerful, doji should catch your eye. Perhaps after the appearance of a doji, a gap of 2% was historically common (the *immediate responsiveness*). It is likely that a gap of this magnitude may occur again if another doji appears. You should also note whether a pattern had an enduring effect (the *effectiveness*). If, in the past, a doji has represented a major turning point, it is likely that if it appears again in the future, the effect will be similar.

THE BEARISH ENGULFING PATTERN

Definition

This two-candle top reversal combination is an extremely effective signal that often dramatically signifies the end of an uptrend, (see Fig. 3.1). While the first candle extends the existing trend, the second real body totally engulfs the first real body and is a bearish sign.

The real body of the second candle opens and closes totally outside the body range of the initial candle. The 'body-to-body' relationship is the critical component. It is a stronger signal if the second candle engulfs the entire range of trading, including the shadows. By definition, engulfing means that no part of the first candle's real body is equal to, or trading outside, the body range of the second candle.

> "...the 'body-to-body' relationship of two-line (or more) candles usually takes precedence over any relationship involving candle shadows."

In some of the figures shown throughout this text, you will see close to perfect examples of the body-to-body relationships that are difficult to replicate exactly in real life. Be aware that if a shadow exists on a share chart, but the body-to-body relationship is intact, then the pattern that you have detected is likely to fulfil the guidelines about the description of that formation.

To summarise, the body-to-body relationship of two-line (or more) candles usually takes precedence over any relationship involving candle shadows. The main exception to this rule involves the tweezer formations, upthrusts and springs, which are formations that will be discussed in Chapter 7.

FIG. 3.1—The Bearish Engulfing Pattern

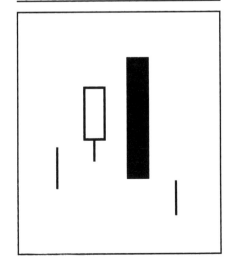

The bearish engulfing pattern requires the first candle to be white and for the second candle to be black. After the appearance of this formation, prices typically plunge steeply.

If you are familiar with traditional Western technical analysis, you may make the error of assessing this pattern as an *outside day*. The predominant difference between an outside day and this formation is that a bearish engulfing pattern compares a body-to-body relationship. An outside day is defined as the trading range of the second period (the low to high of that period) totally enveloping the trading range of the initial period. As with the bearish engulfing pattern, an outside day may be found at the top of a trend. It can also be found at the bottom of a trend, which corresponds to a *bullish engulfing pattern* (which will be discussed next).

Due to the emotional intensity of the open and close, I believe the bearish and bullish engulfing patterns represent the superior definition in comparison to the Western *outside day*. It is also interesting to note that the Japanese analysts isolated this formation a couple of hundred years prior to Western analysts!

Candle Addition

Let's review the process of candle addition with the bearish engulfing pattern as a practical example. When we take the open of candle (1) and the close of candle (2), the real body of candle (3) is formed. The highest high of candle (1) *or* (2) forms the high for candle (3). The lowest low of candle (1) *or* (2) forms the low for candle (3), (see Fig. 3.2).

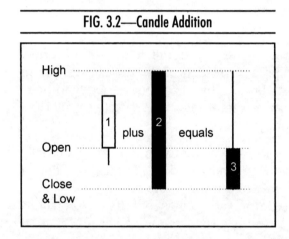

FIG. 3.2—Candle Addition

The bearish engulfing pattern reduces to a formation with a clear bearish direction bias. Depending on the placement of the individual candles, some of these patterns reduce to a fully-formed black shooting star or a gravestone doji. This demonstrates that this type of pattern is unambiguously bearish.

If the process of candle addition resulted in a single candle with bullish tendencies, a far greater level of care would need to be taken at the confirmation phase. Any formations in conflict after the process of candle addition are typically not as strong as those that reduce to a clear, unambiguous one-line candle.

If you come across any new patterns in your travels, the process of candle addition may assist in your understanding of their implications.

Candle Location

Located at the top of a trend, the bearish engulfing pattern is one of the most powerful reversal signals available. Gaps are not usually present before and after the trigger, but this does not nullify the bearish influence. (The trigger candlestick pattern in this case is, of course, both candles (1) and (2).)

Confirmation is derived if prices ultimately trade at a lower range than the second candle. If the next session trades below the mid-point or base of the second candle, this is a particularly bearish sign. The mid-point is defined as being the 50% level of the candle's upper shadow to lower shadow range.

It is interesting to note that when a bearish engulfing pattern has formed to break the uptrend, often a bullish engulfing pattern will be responsible for reversing a downtrend. Many candles have equal, but opposite, counterparts, such as the shooting star and the hammer for example. Often when one of these formations is found at the top of a trend, the counterpart to that pattern will frequently be found at the bottom of the trend for the share.

Psychology

On an emotional level, a devastating blow has been swiftly delivered to the bulls. Those feeling buoyant about the market's upward direction have been proverbially kicked in the teeth. The first period shows that the bulls were still winning the tug of war. The second period, although it initially gaps away from the first body, experiences a quick sell-off. The sell-off is often sustained by high volume, showing that the majority of traders were of a decidedly bearish temperament for the second part of this signal.

The second candle resonates the emotion of fear, as it is usually a long or dominant candle. If volume is a key feature of the activity of the second candle, I consider the second candle to be dominant, rather than long. Future resistance levels are usually found at the base and mid-point of this dominant black candle. Strong bearish patterns such as these often form formidable barriers to future bullish market activity.

THE BULLISH ENGULFING PATTERN

Definition

This candle often signifies the end of a downtrend. The first small black body (which reflects the direction of the trend) is completely engulfed by a long white body, ideally accompanied by a significant volume increase. If the second real body engulfs the shadows of the first day, the pattern will have a higher probability of reversing the trend. The colour of the candle must be black for the first candle and white for the second candle, (see Fig. 3.3, overleaf).

After the pattern has been formed, prices often surge, as buyers move in with enthusiasm.

FIG. 3.3—The Bullish Engulfing Pattern

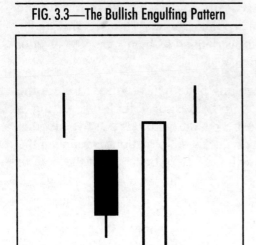

As with its bearish engulfing brother, the second body must totally engulf the first body—and ideally the shadows of the first candle—to obtain maximum impact. Engulfing patterns are very powerful signals.

If the second long white body is accompanied by significant volume, it will form a dominant candle rather than a long candle. The base and mid-point of this candle will serve as a valuable support level for future market activity.

Candle Addition

Figure 3.4 shows the bullish nature of this two-line candle when it is reduced to the one timeframe. This pattern produces a white hammer. Because it reduces to such a strong positive pattern, there is less confirmation required.

If the second candle is exceptionally long, an exaggerated lower shadow is often formed when you apply the process of candle addition. As you know, a lower tail is a sign that buyers are moving in with strength. Therefore, the longer the white candle, the more bullish the pattern. This is especially relevant if this candle starts its life with a significant gap downwards from the first candle.

Candle Location

This engulfing pattern is found at the bottom of a downtrend. Confirmation is derived if subsequent trades are made at least within the range of the second candle, or preferably above the mid-point or entire range.

From experience, I can tell you that the two engulfing patterns often display violent changes of market sentiment. I rarely ignore a signal like this. Trend flattening is not a high probability after the trigger candle. The change in market direction is likely to be immediate and conclusive.

FIG. 3.4—Candle Addition

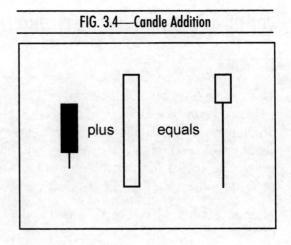

plus   equals

Psychology

The wind has been taken out of the bear's sails, and the bulls have arisen with increased stamina. Traders with short positions make a quick dash to cover their exposure, and their rush to exit their positions adds power to the creation of the pattern. The volume on the uptick component shows that the majority of traders have changed camp from a bearish perspective to a bullish orientation, within the duration of one period. Traders are an emotional bunch, aren't they!

EXAMPLE

There comes a time in every trader's life when they feel completely in tune with the instrument that they are trading. For me, that time was with a series of candles on a BHP chart, (see Fig. 3.5, overleaf). Unfortunately, those magical times rarely last for more than a few weeks at a time!

I enjoy trading the options market, and the series of candlestick patterns shown in Fig. 3.5 enabled me to capture a lovely profit. (Note: The options market allows you to trade where you can benefit from the downtrend, as well as the uptrend.) The engulfing patterns signalled clearly my entries and exits in a manner that I believe is unrivalled by any other type of indicator.

I won't spell out the exact details of the series of trades, but have a look at this chart and marvel at the wonders of the engulfing pattern's detection of turning points. I have also highlighted the evening star for you to have a look at on this chart. We will be discussing this formation further in the next chapter.

FIG. 3.5—BHP Daily

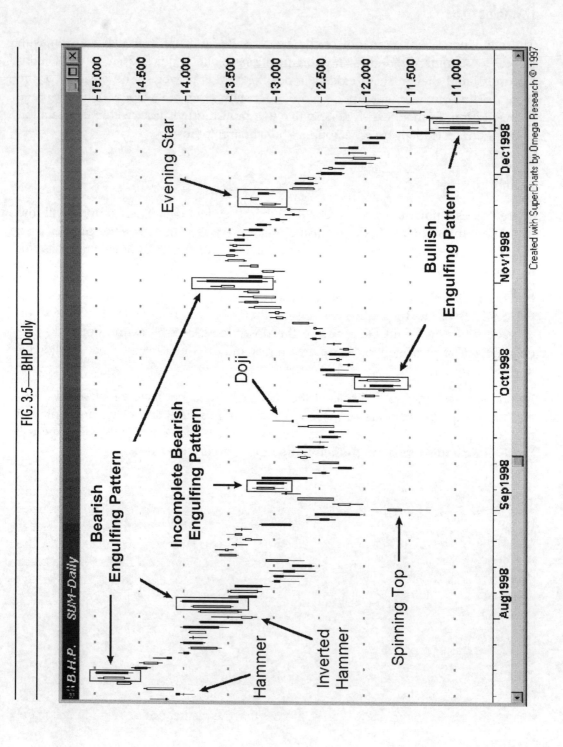

DARK CLOUD COVER

This two-line candle is a top reversal pattern, (see Fig. 3.6). It is especially significant if little, or no, shadows exist. The second black candle must penetrate 50% or more into the body of the initial white candle.

This 50% level of a long candle is the exact point where the bullish tendencies of a subsequent candle are equally matched by the bearish tendencies. The fact that the bears have succeeded in reaching the mid-point of a bullish white candle has shaken the faith of the bulls. As soon as the seesaw is tipped in a bearish direction, this orientation is likely to dominate. For example, penetration of greater than 50% of a black candle into the body of an initial white candle has intense bearish connotations.

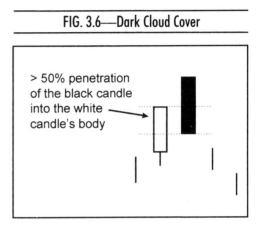

FIG. 3.6—Dark Cloud Cover

> 50% penetration of the black candle into the white candle's body

This pattern is not quite as significant as the bearish engulfing formation. In candlestick philosophy, patterns that are more significant display greater penetration levels of one candle into the body of another. In general, the greater the penetration, the more significant it is.

However, the dark cloud cover is still a very useful signal. When there is dark cloud cover, a downpour may be imminent!

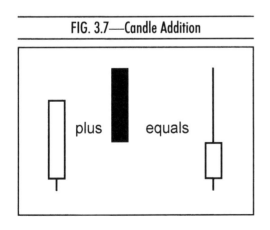

FIG. 3.7—Candle Addition

plus   equals

Candle Addition

The dark cloud cover reduces to a shooting star, (see Fig. 3.7). Notice that this reduced pattern produces a white candle, whereas the reduced formation relating to the bearish engulfing pattern results in a black candle. This assists in explaining why the engulfing pattern implies a stronger bearish reaction.

Candle Location

The first candle extends the existing uptrend, and the second candle runs contrary to the trend. Gaps from the candle prior to the trigger are not common. However, a gap after the trigger in a downward direction reinforces that the market has lost faith in the share.

CBA experienced two back-to-back dark cloud covers just prior to its steep descent into the territory of the bears, (see Fig. 3.8). This type of activity, showing two consecutive dark cloud covers, is not common, and is fundamentally bearish in its intent. At the time of the appearance of these candles, there were few (if any) other indicators telling a bearish story. All signals appeared to be undeniably bullish. The trend was clearly in a long-term upswing. The candle is definitely a leading indicator in comparison to many other analytical tools available.

FIG. 3.8—CBA Daily

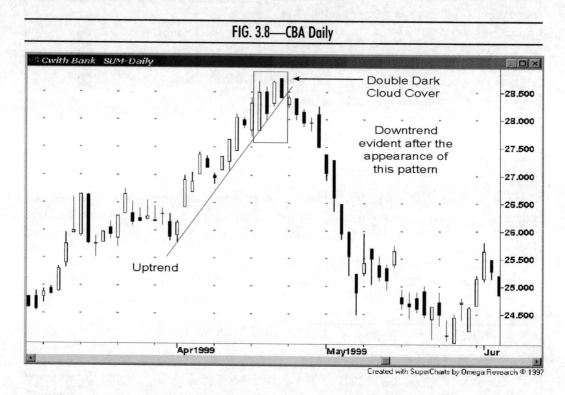

Created with SuperCharts by Omega Research ® 1997

Psychology

The bears have threatened the confidence of the bulls by trading at lower values than the closing price of the first candle. This loss of confidence may lead to a future downturn in trend.

THE PIERCING PATTERN

Definition

This is a two-candle bottom reversal pattern. It is the exact inverse of the dark cloud cover, (see Fig. 3.9). Some texts refer to this as a *piercing white line* or a *piercing line*.

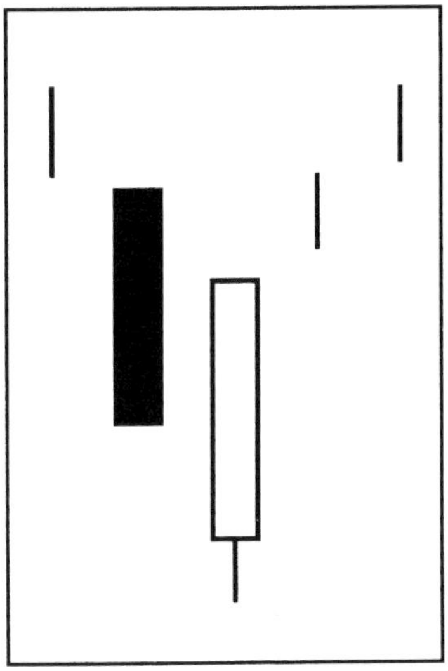

The 50% penetration level of the second candle into the body of the first is *imperative* to the definition.

If you ignore this required level of penetration in your efforts to find an example of this pattern, you might find that you have made a grave error. If there is less than 50% penetration, you will have acted on the basis of a continuation formation, *not* a reversal pattern!

The *on-neck, in-neck* and *thrusting patterns* are all bearish continuation formations with a similar shape to the piercing pattern. The only difference between these patterns and the current formation is that a piercing pattern has 50% or greater penetration levels of the second candle into the body of the first candle. We will not be discussing these related continuation patterns further in this book because there are very few effective examples of them to be found in Australian charts. (Unless I use a candlestick formation on a regular basis in my trading, I am reticent to supply you with a full explanation. This means that you are being exposed to only the most powerful of the patterns as they appear in Australian charts. If you are curious about some of the other candlestick patterns available, you are welcome to refer to the Further Reading section at the back of this book.)

FIG. 3.9—The Piercing Pattern

The piercing pattern is the main formation that has such a very strict definition. Similar continuation patterns related to the dark cloud cover are not available. This is probably due to the fact that market confidence is easily decimated, whereas faith in a share takes a longer time to build. Any sign of a bearish loss of confidence should therefore provide a greater potential for trend reversal, and a minor show of bullish strength will not provide enough momentum to create an uptrend.

To physically throw a ball in the air takes more effort than to watch it effortlessly drop back down to earth. Shares also adhere to this principle. Bulls must show a unified dominating force if they are to lift a share from the depths of bearish influence. In this situation, volume is of paramount importance. It is my view that if insufficient volume is present during a significant directional change from a downtrend to an uptrend, the bullish influence may be short-lived.

Candle Addition

Figure 3.10 (overleaf) shows the bullish nature of this two-candle pattern when it is reduced to the one timeframe. It reduces to a hammer that fully supports a bullish

FIG. 3.10—Candle Addition

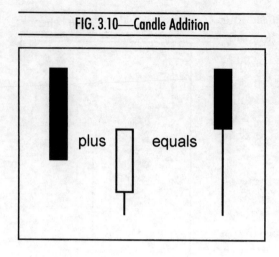

plus   equals

implication. Notice that the colour of the hammer is black, whereas the colour of the reduced bullish engulfing pattern is white. This assists in explaining why the bullish engulfing pattern produces a stronger signal than the piercing pattern.

Candle Location

Piercing patterns are found at the bottom of downtrends. If they are confirmed by higher subsequent prices, they are very reliable. This confirmation is essential in order to trust the implied bullish tendencies.

Psychology

The bears that had been winning the game to date have just been dealt a potentially losing hand. They have been threatened by the traders with bullish tendencies.

The piercing pattern is not as significant as the bullish engulfing pattern. Engulfing patterns totally cover the body of the initial candle and this characteristic intensifies the likelihood of a reversal.

HARAMI

Description

The harami is one of the few patterns that permits two of the same coloured candles to appear side by side. Whether a white and a white candle are present, a black and a black candle, or whether candles of opposite colour are represented, the implication is the same. The trend will either reverse or soften into a sideways trend.

To my knowledge, the only other patterns that tolerate the appearance of two of the same-coloured candles are patterns that are defined by the shadow location only, not the placement of real bodies. An example of a pattern fitting this description is the *tweezer top* (discussed in Chapter 7).

In many ways, the harami looks like an engulfing pattern in reverse. The first real body must totally engulf the second real body in order to form a harami. If the shadows are also engulfed, this forms an even more powerful signal, (see Fig. 3.11).

The premise behind this is that the market is taking a break from the direction of the initial candle. The market is pausing for a period of recovery. It is not unusual to see a sideways trend occur after the appearance of a harami, as it does not generate the powerful counter-trend signal of an engulfing pattern. Often, the trend can be seen to soften, rather than violently change direction.

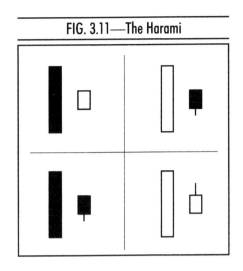

FIG. 3.11—The Harami

Candle Addition

Because of the differences in colour permitted within the definition of a harami between the first and second body, the process of candle addition is less relevant.

Candle Location

Harami are both top and bottom reversal signals. They have bullish tendencies when found at the bottom of trends, and bearish tendencies when found at the top of trends.

Confirmation consists of a subsequent candle trading within the span of the initial real body. This will signal that a sideways movement is likely. If the trading of the periods following the harami show movement of share prices outside the range of the initial body, counter to the existing trend, the signal is also considered to be confirmed. A violent reversal is not unilaterally expected with a harami.

Psychology

The first real body is long in nature and represents a decided move by the market in one direction. The second real body shows indecision, as it is small in relation to the first real body. This indecision shows vulnerability to a counter-trend attack. Dominating strength is required to continue a trend, and the opposing team usually acts upon any sign of weakness.

At first glance, the harami resembles an *inside day* (as defined by Western analysis techniques). The main difference between an inside day and this pattern is that a harami compares a body-to-body relationship. An inside day is defined as the trading range of the first period (the low to high of that period) totally enveloping the trading range of the second period. Due to the emotional intensity of the open and close, I believe the harami represents the superior definition.

HARAMI CROSS

Description

The harami cross is related to the harami. It consists of an initial long real body that totally engulfs the trading range of the subsequent doji, (see Fig. 3.12). Remember that a doji day is where the open and close are approximately equal, indicating a period of indecision. The greater the indecision, the greater the likelihood of reversal. This means that a harami cross is a stronger signal than the harami.

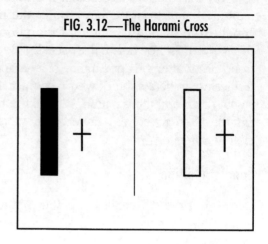

FIG. 3.12—The Harami Cross

The first candle is usually true to the direction of the original trend, therefore a black harami cross is a bottom reversal pattern (the first image in Fig. 3.12), and a white harami cross is a top reversal pattern (the second image in Fig. 3.12). This may not always be the case, but in my observations, this is more common than a colour opposite to the predominant trend appearing as the initial candle.

Candle Addition

The white harami cross reduces to a signal that shows clear rejection of higher prices. Its bearish intent is unmistakable. The black harami cross reduces to a hammer, and it shows a pattern where buyers have now moved into this share with strength, (see Fig. 3.13).

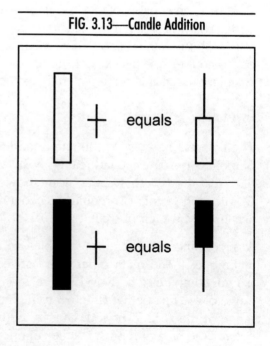

FIG. 3.13—Candle Addition

Note that the colours of the reduced patterns do not provide a signal with the clarity of the engulfing patterns. For example, a bullish engulfing pattern produces a white hammer which adds to the bullish impulse of the future price direction. This implies that the harami and harami cross are not as powerful as the engulfing patterns.

If you notice a harami cross of a different colour variation to the description that I have provided, you should pay attention to it, and watch for confirmation prior to acting. This variation in interpretation is derived primarily from my own observations.

Candle Location

A white harami cross is a top reversal pattern, so it will be found at the top of uptrends. The black harami cross is a bottom reversal pattern. Confirmation is the same as for the common harami.

Psychology

The first long real body is usually a clear sign of market decisiveness. The second body shows that the market has lost its way, and neither the bulls nor the bears are dominating.

An interesting detail to note is that if a strong move above a previous level of resistance or below a strong level of support has occurred the market is likely to pause and consolidate, prior to resuming its vigorous trending behaviour. A harami or harami cross often represents the ideal resting point for a tired market. The share is much more likely to pause for a cool drink prior to commencing its bullish or bearish run.

An indication that this may be the case is if the second small body incurs a significant volume surge. The market is 'churning' as new buyers buy, and sellers who have been in the sideways moving share begin selling. There is a lot of activity in the share, but neither the bull's team nor the bear's team is winning. These sellers have become bored with the share, so they wait for a suitable uptick to sell. So many times I have heard novices say: "Once that share gets to $3.00, I'll sell the damn thing! That horrible share has headed south from the day I bought it!" Waiting for a share to go up in value to sell is often a futile exercise as traders may be in for a very long wait. They've also tied up two valuable resources—capital and their brain cells—while waiting for this eventuality. When an upward movement occurs, they cannot believe their luck so they rush the market with their shares. Many shares change hands in this situation and volume is the key signal. If you notice this happen, and you have a current position in the share, it will often pay dividends to wait before you sell. Higher prices may be on their way.

Figure 2.12 on page 35 shows an exact example of this scenario. A harami cross was formed above a previous line of resistance. The cross component of the formation showed a huge increase in volume. After this brief pause, the share then dramatically trended upwards, as the bulls began to dominate. In this situation, it is very unlikely that a reversal pattern will cause anything but a momentary pause. It is important to examine the lead-up in order to assess whether the implication will result in a reversal or a continuation. The lead-up in Fig. 2.12 was more likely to favour a continuation of the bullish uptrend, even though a classically diagnosed reversal was apparent.

Have a look at Fig. 3.14 (opposite). There are examples in this chart of many of the candlesticks that you have learned about so far. It is interesting to note that the harami crosses shown on this chart did not have a significant trend-reversing effect. This is because they are located on the top of an *insignificant* uptrend. For a candle to be most effective as a reversal, the trend must be well-defined and last for several periods. The harami found on this chart had a clear impact on trend reversal, as did the piercing pattern. The share had been clearly trending, so these reversal patterns performed their role with precision.

OTHER INSTRUMENTS

Even though I have been focusing on the analysis of equities so far in this book, candlesticks are applicable to a wide variety of sharemarket instruments. As long as there is enough volume to create a meaningful pattern, you can use candles to trade futures, options, warrants, shares or CFDs.

CFDs are 'Contracts for Difference'. They have literally caused a trading revolution. Traders have flocked to this new tool to gain access to leverage, and develop the ability to go long and short on a variety of tools. (Going long enables you to profit from an uptrend, and going short allows you to profit from a downtrend.) The main tool utilised when trading CFDs is the ASX top 200 shares. Other possibilities include CFDs on stock market indices, foreign exchange and metals.

CFDs allow you to deal on share prices without having to physically settle on the trade. With CFDs you are trading a contract that represents the share. This has many benefits. To learn more about these fascinating tools, listen to my double CD set called *Power Trading—Trade CFDs Like a Professional*, available from my website.

It's important to keep up to date on the latest trading techniques. If you would like to register for a free monthly email newsletter written by Chris Tate and me, as well as receive a free trading plan review to help you formulate your own trading plan, register your details at www.tradingsecrets.com.au.

Take some time now to cement your knowledge and complete the review section on the following pages.

FIG. 3.14—Boral Daily

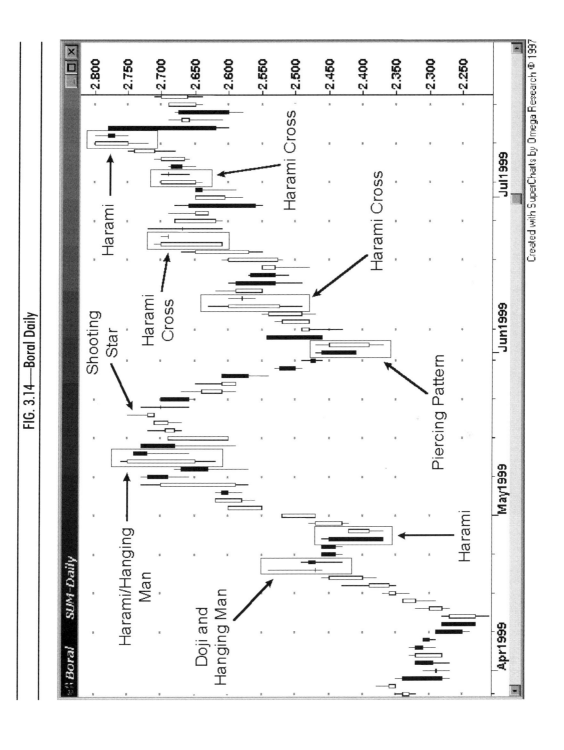

REVIEW

1) Which of the patterns in Fig. 3.15 is a piercing pattern, (a) or (b)?

FIG. 3.15—Which One is a Piercing Pattern?

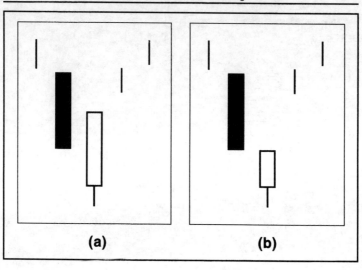

(a)   **(b)**

FIG. 3.16—Pattern Recognition

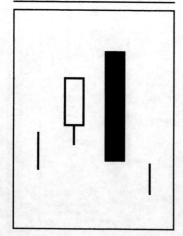

2) What is the pattern in Fig. 3.16? Is it bullish or bearish?

_____

_____

3) A harami cross is less significant than a harami:

(a) True   (b) False

4) Candle addition takes the open of the initial candle and the close of the final candle to form the real body of a single candle:

(a) True   (b) False

5) Have a look at Fig. 3.17 (opposite). Identify and define the main candlestick patterns on this chart.

FIG. 3.17—Lend Lease Daily

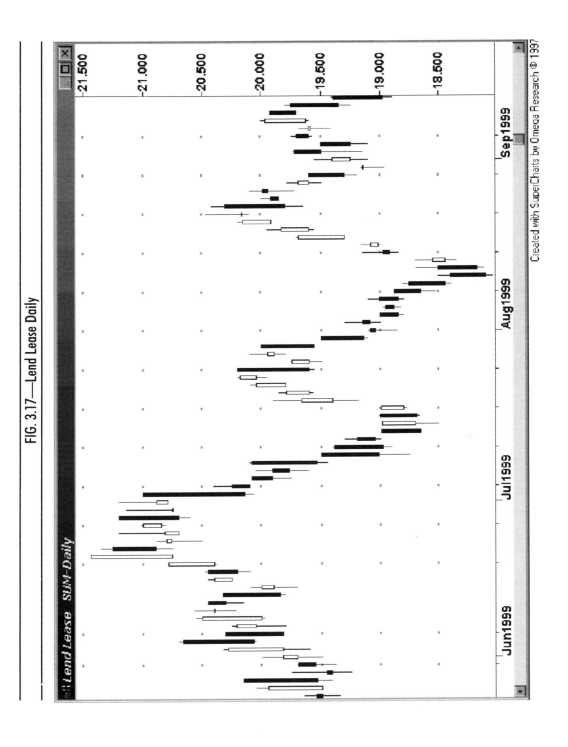

ANSWERS

1) (a) is the correct answer. The white body of the second candle must penetrate the initial body by 50% or greater. If the level of penetration is less than 50%, the pattern is actually defined as a continuation. A continuation formation has the exact opposite implication of a reversal pattern.

2) This is a bearish engulfing pattern. The second black real body totally engulfs the first smaller white body. It has a powerful bearish effect.

3) (b) False. Any candlestick signal combined with a doji becomes *more* powerful. The doji forms the 'cross' part of a harami cross signal. The doji represents the ultimate state of indecision. Any sign of indecision shows potential for a reversal. The share must be clearly trending for any reversal pattern to be effective.

4) (a) True. Candle addition is the process of adding separate candles together to produce a single candlestick. The initial and the final candle provide the data for the real body, and the overall high and overall low form the shadows of the newly-created single candle.

5) See Fig. 3.18 (opposite) for suggested answers. You may have found other patterns on the chart in addition to those I have indicated. This is perfectly acceptable. Even though I have sought throughout this book to quantify and measure each pattern, the art of recognising the implications of candlesticks is somewhat subjective.

→ → → *Now that you have had a look at some powerful two-line candles, add to your knowledge by studying three-line formations...* → → →

FIG. 3.18—Lend Lease Daily

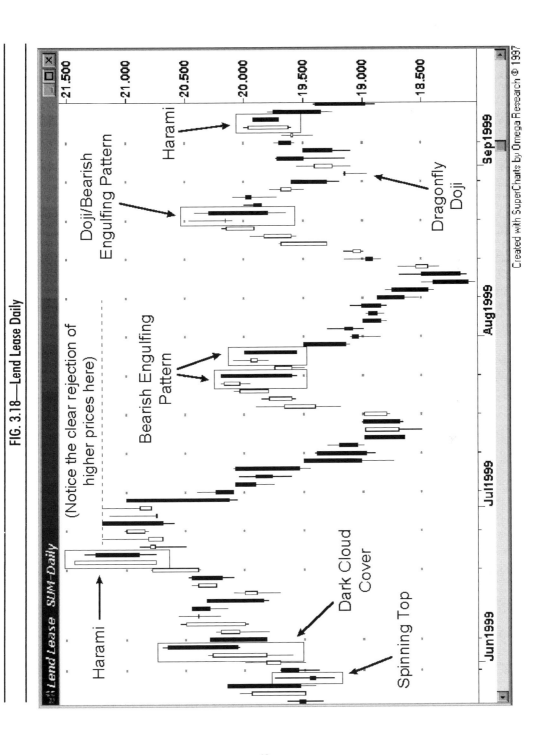

Chapter 4

THREE-LINE CANDLE REVERSAL PATTERNS

Some candlestick formations consist of three separate candles. It is important to note that just because a formation includes *more* candles, it does not necessarily mean that it has a greater potential to reverse the trend. Each pattern, regardless of the number of separate candles that it involves, has a varying level of strength. The power of each pattern depends on the lead-up to the appearance of the trigger, the confirmation phase, and whether the candlestick has had a predictable effect on the share in the past.

For each pattern, we will discuss the trigger, the implications of candle addition, the ideal location, as well as the psychology of the market that produced the signal.

The lessons that you learned about candle addition also hold true for three-line patterns. The process of candle addition is necessary to establish the level of confirmation required after a signal has occurred.

When you begin trading using candlestick methods, you may have to spend some time getting to know your shares in relation to candlesticks. Remember to use a daily chart, as well as a weekly chart, during this process. Some patterns, which occur with regularity on a daily chart, may be totally absent on a weekly chart of the same share. If you have access to intra-day candlestick charts, they can also reveal some incredible secrets about the behavioural characteristics of the share.

With exchange-traded options, I tend to focus on the analysis of approximately 12 shares. The options related to these shares have high levels of buyer and seller activity, so they provide a suitable vehicle to trade. I have come to recognise the signals that are likely to trigger reversal in each of the 12 shares, and this allows me to trade with a higher probability of success. (These shares are listed in _The Secret of Writing Options_, by Louise Bedford, Wrightbooks, 1999.)

THE EVENING STAR

Description

This bearish three-candle reversal shows a long white real body (1), a small star of either colour (2), then a black real body (3), (see Fig. 4.1). The black candle (3) may close within the body of the white candle (1), preferably after a gap from the star (2).

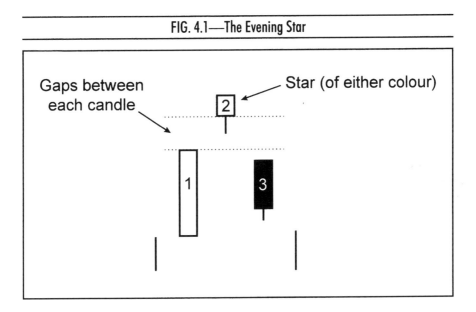

FIG. 4.1—The Evening Star

The lower the black candle (3), the more significant the implication. If the black body (3) closes with a gap down from the initial white candle (1), it will also fulfil the definition of an evening star. The evening star is especially potent if there are gaps between each candle. It is a very powerful top reversal pattern and it can be observed with surprising regularity.

Some analysts define candle (1) and (2) only as an evening star, rather than taking candle (3) into consideration. These analysts refer to the full three candles as a _three-river evening star_. Personally, I prefer to consider the evening star as a three-line candle, rather than a two-line candle, so we will be using this terminology throughout the book. The third candle of the pattern provides a bearish confirmation of the previous two candles, so I feel that I can rely on the trend-reversal power of the three candles to a greater degree.

Candle Addition

Let's run through the process of candle addition as it relates to a three-candle pattern. To reduce a three-candle pattern to a single candle, take the opening price of candle (1) and the closing price of candle (3) to form the real body of the reduced candle. The highest point of candle (1), (2) or (3) will form the upper shadow of the newly-formed candle. The lowest price of candle (1), (2) or (3) is used to form the lower shadow, (see Fig. 4.2).

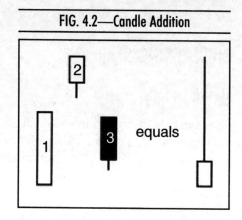

FIG. 4.2—Candle Addition

The evening star reduces to a shooting star, which has a decidedly bearish implication. Depending on the location of the third candle, the evening star will reduce to either a white or a black shooting star. This fully supports the evening star as being a powerful top reversal signal.

Candle Location

An evening star is located at the top of a trend, and rather than creating a softening of trading activity, a dramatic direction change will often ensue. When the gaps are distinct between each candle, this is one of the strongest signals available.

If candle (3) is located below the body of candle (1) or opens within the lower 50% and closes below the body of candle (1), this suggests an immediate hostile take-over bid by the bears, especially when high volume is present on the third candle. Candle addition of this type of pattern will produce a black shooting star. This will also produce a more forceful downtrend than the evening star shown in Fig. 4.2.

In the chart of AMP (see Fig. 4.3, opposite), two evening stars heralded the dramatic end to the separate uptrends. From this analysis, we could put forward the hypothesis that AMP is 'responsive' to the evening star. As a bottom reversal, we could assume that AMP is responsive to bullish engulfing patterns and harami (although further back-testing is suggested to make this claim with absolute assuredness). If this is our hypothesis, then future detection of these formations would suggest that there is a high probability that the appearance of a new evening star, a harami, or a bullish engulfing pattern would be equally as effective. This would allow less stringent levels of confirmation required in the future, so hasty action could be taken to enter or exit our positions once these signals appear again. This type of analysis will give you an edge over other traders.

FIG. 4.3—AMP Daily

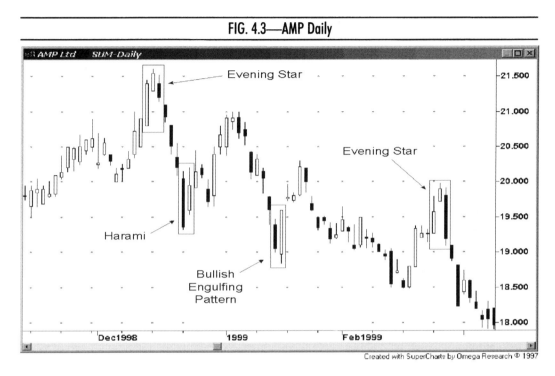

Created with SuperCharts by Omega Research ℗ 1997

Confirmation of the evening star is easy to recognise. Future trading activity should be at least below the mid-point of the final candle in order to provide confirmation that the trend has changed to a downward direction. This concept of a mid-point is further explained when we discuss the implications of the morning star (which is the next signal on the agenda.)

After the appearance of an evening star, a gap downward to the next trading session will often occur. This is more common than a subsequent candle closing within the body of the final candle of the evening star.

Psychology

The first candle reflects a clear bullish direction. The bulls are making a run and it seems nothing can stop them. A gap upward from this initial candle reinforces the bullish sentiment, but this session quickly turns to a period of indecision, as depicted by a small candle. The indecision shakes the confidence of the bulls, so the bears move in with strength to create the final candle. The impulse to sell overrides the trader's predisposition towards greed.

The morning star is next on our agenda. This pattern directly shows the impact of the emotion of greed on a market.

THE MORNING STAR

Description

This bullish three-candle bottom reversal shows a long black real body (1), a small star of either colour (2), then a white real body (3), (see Fig. 4.4). As with most candlestick reversals, it is especially significant with gaps between each candle.

FIG. 4.4—The Morning Star

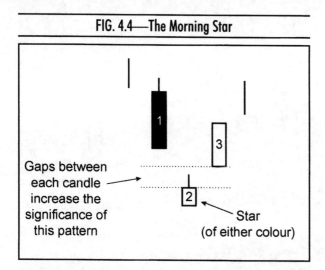

Gaps between each candle increase the significance of this pattern

Star (of either colour)

In this formation, the white candle (3) usually closes within the body of the black candle (1) or above, preferably after a gap from the star (2). The higher the white candle (3), the more bullish the implication. I personally prefer to see an increase in volume coinciding with the appearance of candle (3). In order to shake the bulls out of their depression, and to buoyantly drive up the share price, volume is a positive and necessary sign.

With any pattern showing bullish tendencies, I feel that a significant increase in volume is necessary. Imagine that you were pushing a boulder up a hill. It would take a lot more effort to push the boulder up the incline than it would to allow it to roll back down the hill. The energy expended is similar to the effort that it takes to drive a share price up in value. Volume is required to ensure that there are enough other decisive bulls in the market prepared to put their money where their mouth is.

As with the evening star, some analysts prefer to consider the first two candles to be defined as the morning star. These analysts would define the three-line candle as a *three-river morning star*. As I prefer the bullish confirmation of the third candle, I have always considered the morning star to be composed of three candles. Throughout this book, we will continue with the definition of the morning star consisting of three lines.

FIG. 4.5—Candle Addition

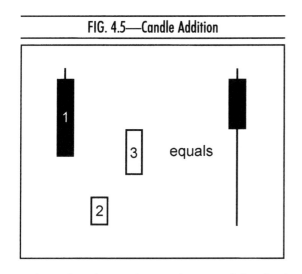

Candle Addition

The morning star reduces to a hammer, which fully supports the bullish impact of the morning star, (see Fig. 4.5). The placement of the final candle in this pattern will determine whether the formation reduces to a white or a black hammer.

Candle Location

The morning star is a bottom reversal pattern. Future trading activity should at least be above the *mid-point* of the final candle in order to provide confirmation that the trend has changed to an upward direction.

As you will remember, the mid-point is defined as being the 50% level of the candle's upper shadow to lower shadow range. Some candles are more receptive to mid-point analysis than others. Shaven candles that represent long or dominant days are the most likely candidates. Any candle with a significant shadow is unlikely to be receptive to this type of analysis.

The mid-point represents the shift of power from a bullish perspective to a bearish perspective, and vice versa. Basically, any penetration into a dominant or long candle of greater than 50% by a candle of the opposite colour has significant trend-reversal implications. It is a concept widely used in many candlestick formations; for example, the dark cloud cover and piercing pattern.

Psychology

The bears are about to be sent into hibernation by the bulls. The downward direction of the initial candle is followed by a period of indecision. The final bullish candle sends ripples of greed throughout the trading community, especially when accompanied by significant volume levels.

Figure 4.6 (overleaf) shows an example of the bullish nature of this pattern. News Corporation had experienced a sustained downtrend. This trend was reversed by the appearance of a perfectly-formed morning star.

Notice how all subsequent trading activity after the appearance of the morning star stays above the mid-point of the long white candle. This is a significant observation. Powerful bottom reversals such as the morning star often provide a clue regarding the future levels of support that can be expected. Support will often form at the mid-point of long or dominant candles. Gaps also provide a barrier that proves difficult for the bears to penetrate. We will be discussing the concept of support and resistance in greater detail in Chapters 6 and 7.

FIG. 4.6—News Corporation Daily

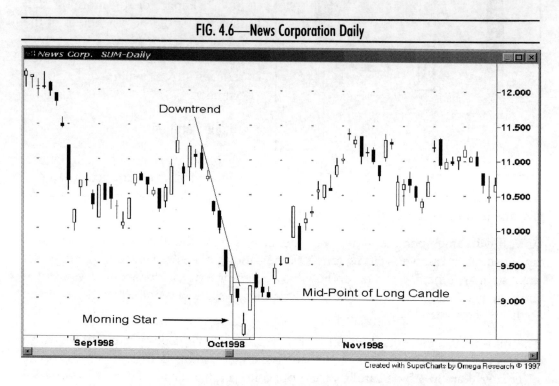

Created with SuperCharts by Omega Research ® 1997

THE EVENING AND MORNING DOJI STARS

Description

Whenever a doji is combined with any pattern, the power of that formation is intensified. When a doji forms the second candle of a morning or evening star, the possibility of a reversal increases. The session after the doji, which is a part of the entire formation, should confirm the impending trend reversal, (see Figs. 4.7 and 4.8, opposite).

The signals shown in Figs. 4.7 and 4.8 comply with the definition of an *abandoned baby* pattern. The only difference between an abandoned baby, and a evening/morning doji star is that the doji must gap totally away from the candle range of candle (1) and candle (3). For those of you familiar with standard Western technical analysis, this is similar to a single-bar *island reversal day*.

The abandoned baby is quite rare, so we will not dwell on this, suffice to say that it is an advanced form of the evening/morning doji star. The powerful reversal implications of an abandoned baby suggest that you should never ignore it if you come across one. In my analysis, I tend to not distinguish between an abandoned baby and an evening or morning doji star. Their implications are similar, and this is all that I am concerned about in my trading activities.

Candle Addition

The candle addition reduces to the same patterns evident for the evening and morning star, (see Figs. 4.2 and 4.5).

Candle Location

All the guidelines you have learned in relation to the morning and evening star are relevant when a doji forms the star.

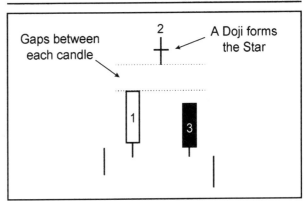

FIG. 4.7—The Evening Doji Star

Gaps between each candle

A Doji forms the Star

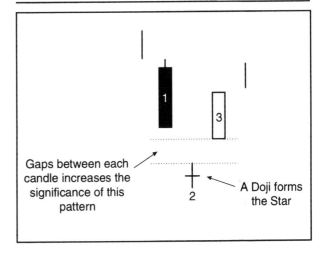

FIG. 4.8—The Morning Doji Star

Gaps between each candle increases the significance of this pattern

A Doji forms the Star

Psychology

The doji represents a heightened level of indecision by the market. Whenever this level of indecision is present, there is a strong likelihood of a reversal in trend.

Regardless of the strength of any candlestick, the impact is only likely to be short-term in nature. Have a look at Fig. 4.9 (overleaf). The bearish intent of the evening doji star served to only halt the momentous bullish uptrend for a few periods. The uptrend flattened for a while, but then resumed.

At a later date in the chart of BHP, however, the evening star and morning doji stars had an effect of total and undeniable trend reversal, (see Fig. 4.10, overleaf). Notice how the morning doji star depicted fulfils our precise definition? Although some latitude is allowed in definitions, it is refreshing to observe a perfectly-formed pattern when it does occur.

FIG. 4.9—BHP Daily

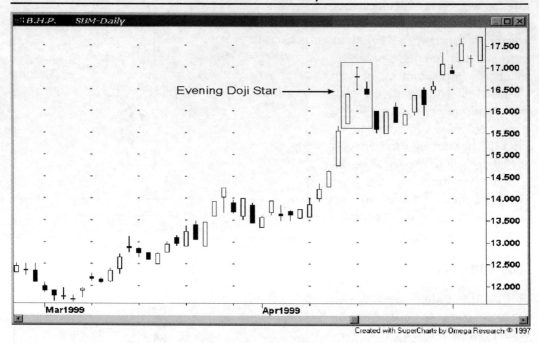

Evening Doji Star →

Created with SuperCharts by Omega Research ® 1997

FIG. 4.10—BHP Daily

Evening Star

Morning Doji Star →

Created with SuperCharts by Omega Research ® 1997

Figure 4.10 shows an example of how one pattern with an opposite counterpart can be responsible for an uptrend reversal, and then a downtrend reversal. The evening star reversed the uptrend, and its related counterpart, the morning doji star, reversed the downtrend. This type of symmetrical counterpart formations working on a chart at opposite ends of the trend is almost mystical to observe. It is like two graceful, agile dancers moving together, a perfect complement to each other. Not only aesthetically pleasing, it also provides powerful clues to perceptive traders regarding how to benefit from candlestick analysis.

TWO CROWS

Definition

Even though this is called two crows, it is actually a three-line top reversal pattern. It is related to the evening star.

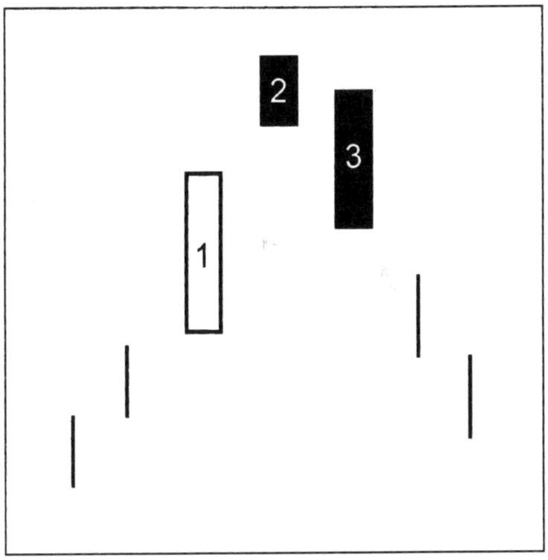

The existing trend is extended with the appearance of the initial white candle. An upward gapping black day is formed which typically has a smaller body than the initial white candle. The third session opens within the body of the second candle and it closes below the close of the initial candle, (see Fig. 4.11). If the close of the final candle was above the close of the initial candle it would be called an *upside gap two crows*. This pattern is also a top reversal pattern.

Some analysts may define the evening star shown in Fig. 4.10 as being a two crows pattern. As a star with a very small body formed the central candle, I chose to define it as an evening star. Regardless

FIG. 4.11—Two Crows

of your definition, the bearish confirmation of the pattern determined that it was indeed a reversal signal.

Candle Addition

The two crows reduces to the same shape as shown by the evening star in Fig. 4.2. This supports the bearishness of this formation.

Candle Location

This is a bearish reversal that only occurs while an instrument is in uptrend. The longer the second black day and the lower it closes into or under the body of the initial white candle, the more bearish the pattern.

Confirmation is derived from a subsequent candle trading within the range of the first white candle, or below the body of this initial candle.

Psychology

When you compare candles (1) and (3) in Fig. 4.11, it is evident that the share has experienced a lower close. This has shaken the bulls' level of confidence. The bears are about to move in for the kill.

The crow is regarded by the Japanese as a sinister bird. Much of Japanese folklore is based on superstitions regarding this creature. There are many other bearish patterns that are named after this bird. We will not be discussing each of these other patterns, as there are only infrequent effective examples of them in Australian charts.

Shortcut

If you are struggling with the recognition and detection of some patterns, understand that candlestick analysis is an acquired skill. It will take time and dedication to conquer. I promise you that it will be worth your effort! You will be paid according to your ability to detect trends and turning points, so the time that you commit to learning this new skill will pay dividends.

When I first learned the art of candlestick charting, I found that it helped to run a line through the general direction of the trend by connecting the approximate mid-points of each of the candles present. I call this line a *trend direction line*. It is not actually a trendline. (A traditional trendline will connect the highest highs for a downtrend, and the lowest lows for an uptrend. The purpose of a trendline is to show when a trend is in place, and to watch for a break in the trend which will be apparent when the share prices cross over the line.) Once some trend direction lines are drawn, I then look at the peaks and the troughs formed by these lines to see whether any significant candles were present at the turning points.

This is perhaps easier to explain by using an example. Have a look at the chart in Fig. 4.12 (opposite). You will notice that I have drawn a line through the general trend of the share, then I have reviewed the chart to see if any meaningful candlestick formations were present at each turning point of the line. This may assist in your efforts to establish the correct location of possible candlestick patterns. You may find that the trick of drawing in a trend direction line will assist your efforts in developing the valuable skill of pattern detection.

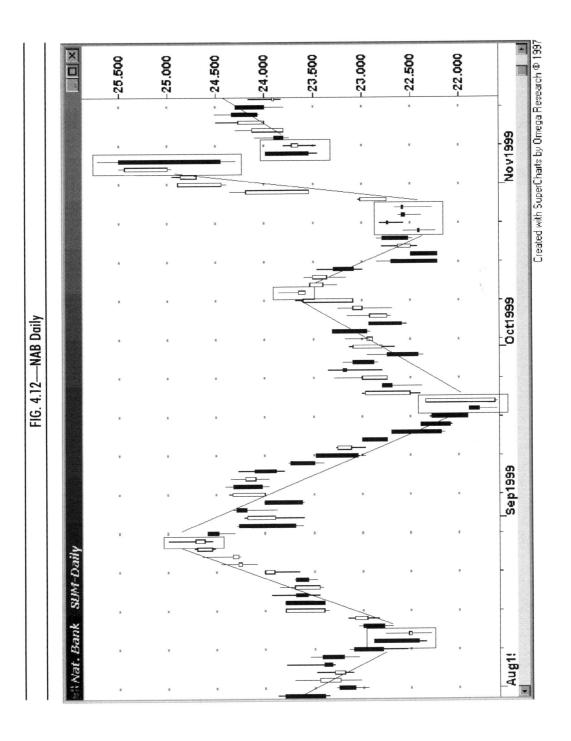

FIG. 4.12—NAB Daily

REVIEW

1) As a general rule, top reversal patterns require less confirmation than bottom reversals:

(a) True   (b) False

2) The *evening doji star* is a top reversal pattern that has greater strength than *the evening star*:

(a) True   (b) False

3) Have a look at Fig. 4.12. Try to name each of the candlestick patterns that have been isolated for you. Did these patterns successfully reverse the trend of the share?

ANSWERS

1) (a) True. Top reversals require less confirmation because the market can quickly lose faith in a share, and therefore experience dramatic downward corrections. With bottom reversals, I prefer to see an increase in volume, as well as heightened levels of confirmation prior to acting on the signal provided by the bottom reversal candlestick.

2) (a) True. Any candlestick with a doji forming the star will be stronger than if a star with a larger real body formed the pattern. The doji represents the ultimate balance of buyer and seller demand. As such, it increases the probability of a trend reversal.

3) See Fig. 4.13 (opposite) for answers to the pattern recognition test.

If you would like a handy quick reference guide to help you remember the main candlestick patterns, you may want to pick up *The Secret of Candlestick Charting* Poster. *The Secret of Pattern Detection* Poster is also available via www.tradingsecrets.com.au. These posters will help you to use candlesticks in conjunction with western macro patterns.

→ → → *We have covered my favourite candlestick reversals, so it's now time to move on to how candles can assist in detecting when a trend is likely to continue. Keep reading to learn about candlestick continuation patterns...* → → →

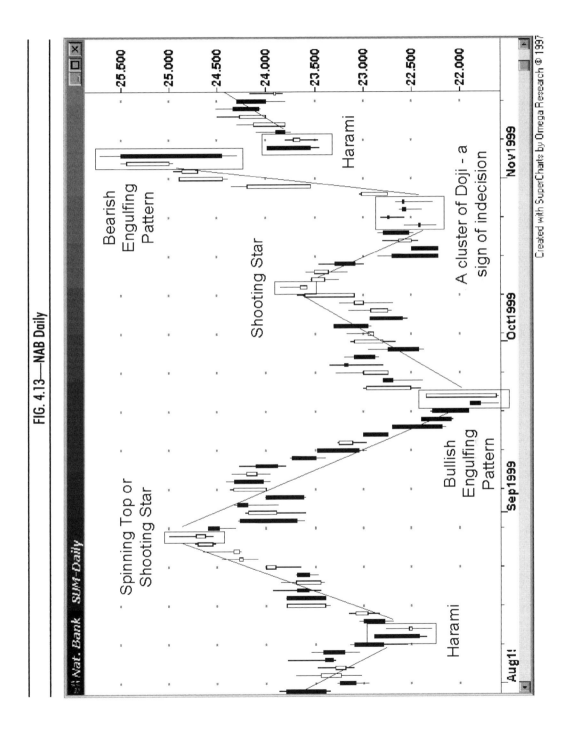

FIG. 4.13—NAB Daily

Chapter 5

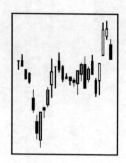

TRADING CONCEPTS AND CONTINUATION PATTERNS

In this chapter we are going to look at continuation patterns. However, before we do this, let's look a bit more closely at the main components of a successful trade:

- ➥ Opportunity identification
- ➥ Placing the order
- ➥ Money and risk management.

We will discuss each of these issues in turn. For more information on this topic, complete my *Candlestick Charting Home Study Course* or watch *The Secret of Candlestick Charting* Video Program available through www.tradingsecrets.com.au.

OPPORTUNITY IDENTIFICATION

As traders, we must first identify appropriate trading opportunities. How do we find opportunities with a high probability of bringing in future profits? You will need to develop your own system of trading which defines entry and exit points, has clear rules for money and risk management, and provides guidelines about how you will react to predetermined scenarios. This valuable foundation must be established prior to entering the trade.

I suggest that candlesticks are included in your trade identification process. However, I would strongly encourage you not to make them the only basis. Look for the weight of evidence that other analytical methods can supply to confirm your entry and exit decisions made by candlestick analysis. This will result in a far higher probability of winning trades.

"After a candlestick signal, I suggest that you take action within the next two to three sessions…"

If you already have a system that is working for you, I caution you against altering the methods that you are currently using. As traders we will often experience periods where profits appear to be quite elusive. During these phases it is extremely tempting to deviate from an established system in search of a superior method. This is a very dangerous practice. Every trader loses money from time to time. It is the way that we recover from these losses that can make the difference between making an overall loss and being a trader who finishes the year in a net profit position.

PLACING THE ORDER

This refers to the method that you will use to actually open your initial transaction, and to exit your position. For example, you may prefer the comfort of actually speaking to a broker and receiving verbal confirmation that your trade has been executed. Other traders may find that processing orders via the Internet represents the ideal situation for their requirements.

Whichever system you choose must take into account the term of your trade. For example, if you are a day trader, you will want immediate broker attention whenever you call. Your broker must not show the slightest hesitation when placing the order, otherwise a perfectly good trading opportunity may be lost for the whole day. Perhaps you will also need to consider a contingency plan if you cannot contact your broker in time to process your order.

If the term of your trade is medium- to long-term, the execution may not be as desperate. Your broker may perform the transaction at any time of the day, and still fulfil your execution requirements.

After a candlestick signal, I suggest that you take action within the next two to three sessions, otherwise the impact will not be as potent. For example, if you have been basing your trading decisions on an intra-day candlestick chart with a time increment of five minutes, then execution of your trades must take this into account. If an appropriate signal on a five-minute chart is generated, then you must take action within approximately the next five to fifteen minutes, or the trading opportunity may not be as favourable. The impact of a confirmed candlestick pattern will last approximately one to ten periods. If you miss the signal, or if you are sloppy at executing, then do not make the trade. He who hesitates is lost.

The shortest time increment that I tend to use on a candlestick chart is ten minutes. In order for a candlestick chart to be beneficial when using this style of intra-day chart, the instrument must have sufficient volume and volatility. If it does not, all you will see on the candle chart will be a series of blanks or horizontal lines depicting that there was minimal activity for that period.

A horizontal line on a candlestick chart can mean that the open, high, low and close are all at the same price. When this occurs, it is called a *four-price doji*. Usually a horizontal line means that there was minimal trading volume for that period. Some charting packages that use end-of-day data show a four-price doji even if there was no trade for that period. (On a share that is usually volatile, this may mean that the instrument has been placed on suspension and will not be allowed to trade until a particular announcement has been made.) If you suspect that you have located a genuine four-price doji, refer to volume to ensure that there were actually some trades represented in that period. If you have access to a real-time candlesticks system, four-price doji are very common on shares with low liquidity on tight time increments.

The other principle involved in this stage of successful share trading is the ability to 'pull the trigger'. If you have identified a set-up that is in line with your entry rules, then you must enter the trade—otherwise you have an interesting hobby, rather than a lucrative income-generating activity. 'Trading' is a verb, or an action word. Rather than passively observing, you will learn lessons regarding the market with astounding speed if you actually enter a trade, even if it is only with a small amount of money initially. Paper trading will only take you so far. Unless you are willing to take a risk, it is unlikely that your skill as a trader will develop. There are thousands of 'unmarried marriage counsellors' in the trading game that 'talk the talk' but never 'walk the walk'. Vow to never become one of these masses. Commit to action.

MONEY AND RISK MANAGEMENT

This component of trading involves the important areas of position sizing, stop-loss procedures, profit objectives and the psychological impact that trading may have on you. You need to consider these issues before you enter any trading position. Careful prior planning will assist in your trading performance. Analysis of your trade after you have exited your position is also an essential process.

Whenever I have opened a position on the basis of a candlestick pattern, an immediate move in the expected direction provides a great deal of consolation. If an immediate favourable move does not occur, you must make up your mind whether to stay with the trade. The level of 'discomfort' that you are willing to experience should be decided prior to executing the trade. If you make this decision on the spur of the moment, your thought process may be tainted by the fear of watching your profits erode. This does not represent an ideal trading scenario.

The complexity involved in the arena of position sizing is beyond the scope of this book. It is essential to come to grips with the implications of the different position sizing models available, and to assess which model is appropriate for your requirements. Many traders consistently put the same amount of money into each trade, never taking into account the varying nature of the underlying instruments, or realising that a higher return may be available by using an alternative method. The primary text to read on this topic is *Trading Your Way to Financial Freedom* by Dr Van K. Tharp. This is widely considered to be the best book to address this important area. Van Tharp also discusses profit maximisation, psychology, and the concept of expectancy. Expectancy is the overall amount of profit that you make per trade in relation to the overall amount of loss per trade. To calculate your expectancy is strongly suggested as it results in quantifying your true profitability as a trader.

> **"If the trade that I have entered, based on a specific candlestick, does not produce a return within three to five periods, then I exit my position."**

Setting a stop-loss as an exit strategy in order to manage risk is essential. (A stop-loss is the point at which you have been incorrect in your initial view.) If the trade that I have entered, based on a specific candlestick, does not produce a return within three to five periods, then I exit my position. It is essential that the confirmation of a candlestick be derived within the next few periods, otherwise that candle cannot be considered effective. In this situation, there is no basis for holding on to the position in the hope that it will provide a profit. If you do not exit your position, your trade is existing without any foundation, and your capital may be at risk. However, if the trade moves in the expected direction, then I follow my stop-loss rules based on share or option price action. This type of 'time stop' prevents my capital from being needlessly tied up in an inappropriate trade.

In general, for a medium-term trade, I set an initial time and price stop-loss. I then set a trailing stop-loss once the trade is in a profit situation. I trail the stop-loss behind the winning trade going up one support/resistance line at a time, as the share price continues to increase. There are myriad other methods for you to use to lock in your profits.

I pyramid into positions (by adding more capital) as I receive evidence that another breakout has occurred. I pyramid out of positions (by removing capital) at reversals for shorter-term trades, but I always adhere to my absolute price, time and trailing stop-loss. I exit the full position immediately when the share is no longer co-operating with the view that I established prior to entering the trade.

The psychological component of trading is an area widely overlooked by novices. It also happens to be one that separates the expert trader from the mediocre masses. As a trader, it is an area that I am constantly striving to improve upon.

If you have any doubts on an emotional level about your trading strategy, it is likely that your pre-set plans may not be followed during a period of trading pressure. Trading opportunities may be missed due to the foibles of human nature.

The World of the Caveman

A core principle of the sharemarket is that traders should let their profits run and cut their losses. Chris Tate (www.artoftrading.com.au), a well-known author of books on the sharemarket, explained to me that in effect, as a trade becomes more profitable, we should become *risk-seeking* and engage in strategies such as pyramiding. Whereas when a trade goes against us, we should be *risk-averse*, and the trade should be instantly exited.

Unfortunately, many traders have this rule the wrong way around. They become risk-seeking when faced with a loss, and they simply let it run. They are also likely to become risk-averse when a trade is profitable. The old theories of "You'll never go broke taking a profit" or "Leave something on the table for the next person" come into play, and they exit the trade pre-emptively.

It is difficult for traders to obey the rules of trading because their own psychology often defeats them. This concept is far more complex than it would first appear. Perhaps it comes down to the fact that these behaviours have been hardwired into us by evolution. Much of human behaviour is merely a sophisticated replica of the behaviours our ancestors displayed.

Imagine you are one of our primitive ancestors. The world is a frightening place. Virtually everything is bigger, faster and stronger than you are. The only advantage that you have is your ability to think—but thinking is of little value in a life or death struggle. To survive this harsh environment requires a more robust, dynamic behaviour.

Suppose that you are out hunting in the primeval forest, when suddenly, a vicious predator leaps out from behind a tree and attacks. The only behaviour that will offer any survival advantage is to attack, and become risk-seeking. To run would only invite an attack from behind, as your predator is superior in speed.

This is the same behaviour that traders exhibit when faced with a growing loss. The evolutionary behaviour is to attack, to hold on to a trade, or to average down by buying more. In essence, we become risk-seeking. It does not matter that the trader is faced with a losing trade rather than a sabre tooth tiger. The behavioural response is the same. It is to become risk-seeking.

The same behaviour applies to the inability of traders to let profits run. Let's return to our primeval scene and imagine that this time you have come across a bounty. It may be a fruit tree, or a fresh animal carcass. The instinctive behaviour is to grab as much as you possibly can, and then run. In this extraordinarily threatening environment there will always be something bigger, stronger and faster than you nearby. The caveman, like the trader, becomes risk-averse. Whilst we may describe such behaviour in a variety of quaint euphemisms, it is still the same basic behaviour.

The world of our ancestors has also led to a variety of other behaviours that provide impediments to traders. In those ancient times, decisions had to be made rapidly, with limited cognitive input. Classification came before calculus. Is the movement in the bushes simply the wind, or is it something more sinister? The only thing that would ensure survival is a snap judgment. We have transferred this primitive level of thinking to trading.

The popular belief is that trading is a series of snap judgments and instant decisions made in the hostile environment of the market. This thought process also leads to statements such as "BHP is a good share"—the implication is that good shares do the right thing. The right thing means they go up. Unfortunately, this is a primitive classification made by very primitive behaviour.

Trading is a precise and somewhat boring activity, where decisions are made long in advance of any contact with the market. The world's best traders realise this and they plan with meticulous care. Every contingency is considered and reconsidered. This approach may seem boring, and may not appeal to those who believe that trading should be frantically yelling "buy" or "sell" to your broker on a mobile phone while simultaneously admiring the upholstery on your new Porsche.

"My key to developing objectivity is to keep a trading diary." A final behaviour that can lead to our failure is the propensity for traders to listen to gossip and rumour. This is also an evolutionary behaviour. In primitive tribal communities, gossip was the only form of news communication. Those who understood this were able to secure a competitive advantage. This competitive advantage was likely to lead to greater breeding success. Hence, this behaviour was passed on from generation to generation. The desire to listen to gossip and rumour (or to search for the next big tip) is hardwired into us. We are programmed to respond to it. Yet, as traders, it is totally meaningless as a form of behaviour, and effectively works against us.

In trading, our own evolution has conspired against us. The behaviours that in the past ensured our success have, in essence, guaranteed that the majority of people will never make money. The only way to overcome this is through self-awareness. Trading is not about 'feeling right', it is about making money.

My key to developing objectivity is to keep a trading diary. I record all of my thoughts and analysis prior to entering a trade in a two-ring A4 binder. I keep my system rules in this diary, and I refuse to place any trade unless I ensure that the trade complies with every rule. I have a checklist that I complete prior to placing my orders. If there is any variation from my predetermined quantified rules, then I do not enter the trade. If I cannot justify my trade on paper, then I have no logical basis for performing the trade.

Not every trade will co-operate and provide you with a profit. However, if you consider that every trade can be perceived as successful if you learn something about trading, then you have entered the realms of the professional trader.

Every psychological principle that you are experiencing as a trader is also reflected in the entire market's activity. This insight into the mind of the trader is an important feature of candlestick analysis.

CONTINUATION PATTERNS

Let's have a look at some important candlestick continuation patterns. Even though there are not as many available in comparison to reversals, continuation patterns are still an important signal. A continuation pattern implies that the share will continue over the short-term in a specific direction.

UPSIDE TASUKI GAP

Description

The upside tasuki gap occurs when an uptrend is in progress. The initial white candle is followed by an upward gap to the next white candle. The third session shows a black candle that closes into the gap, but does not fully close it. This gap must be present and the final black candle must open within the body of the second session, to strictly adhere to the traditional definition, (see Fig. 5.1).

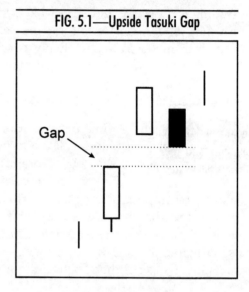

FIG. 5.1—Upside Tasuki Gap

Gap

Candle Addition

The upside tasuki gap reduces to a long line with the white body at the base. A white body is considered to be bullish, suggesting an uptrend continuation. However, the upper shadow suggests potential rejection of higher prices, which indicates a lack of strong bullish support. This is important to note, as you will need to seek confirmation to a greater extent, in comparison to a pattern with a more bullish reduction, (see Fig. 5.2).

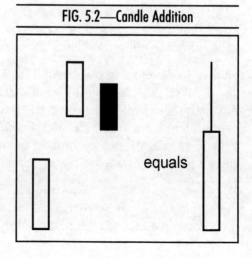

FIG. 5.2—Candle Addition

equals

Candle Location

The share must already be in uptrend prior to the appearance of the trigger candle. The upside tasuki gap is likely to continue this upward trend. Adequate confirmation should involve the next session's trading activity to be maintained above the gap created between the first and the final candle. If this gap is closed, it is unlikely that the uptrend will be sustained in the short term at least.

Psychology

The upside and downside tasuki gap (see below) do not occur frequently. In fact, you may even struggle to find an example of their existence. The main reason I have included this discussion is to illustrate an important point about gap analysis from a candlestick perspective.

Gaps have special importance in candlestick philosophy. As in Western analysis, a gap will indicate a powerful move in market sentiment. It will often form a strong barrier of support or resistance. With this information in mind, if the final bearish candle closes the gap, a change of direction is likely. If the gap was closed, the supportive tendencies would then be eradicated, and the implication would change from bullish to bearish.

It is a positive sign if an instrument pauses, prior to commencing its uptrend, especially after a major push upwards. This pause will often be displayed as a band of consolidation of trading activity, and will in all probability form a base of support which future trading activity is unlikely to penetrate.

Any share that trends at a near-vertical angle, straight up into the heights of blue sky, always concerns me. What goes up, must come down. With trading, often the angle of the uptrend will match the angle of the downward correction. For this reason, a period of sideways consolidation during an uptrend is definitely a healthy sign.

The upside gap tasuki represents a minor pause in the life of an uptrend.

DOWNSIDE TASUKI GAP

Description

This bearish continuation pattern is a counterpart to the upside tasuki gap. The first black day gaps down strongly at the opening of the next session. The second candle is also black. The third candle is white and opens within the body of the second candle. It fails to close the gap formed between the first candle and the second candle, (see Fig. 5.3, overleaf). In effect, this gap acts as a resistance.

Candle Addition

This pattern reduces to a long black line with a black real body located at the top of this line. This is ambiguously bearish. The long lower shadow signifies rejection of lower prices. The black body is bearish, but this long lower shadow should compel you to seek a more stringent form of confirmation prior to acting on the basis of this candlestick, (see Fig. 5.4).

Candle Location

The downside tasuki gap should be located within a downtrend. To signify a reversal, the candle following this pattern should close the gap. If this does not occur, the gap is likely to provide a band of resistance for future trading activity. For this reason, this pattern is likely to extend the existing trend, rather than reverse it.

Psychology

The final candle did not close the gap between the first and the second candle. This suggests that the overall sentiment is still bearish. If the gap were to be closed in future trading sessions, the downside tasuki gap would no longer have a bearish connotation.

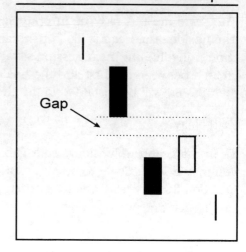

FIG. 5.3—The Downside Tasuki Gap

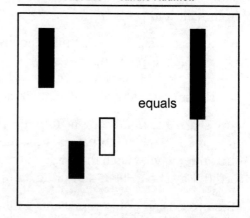

FIG. 5.4—Candle Addition

RISING THREE METHOD

Description

This is a continuation pattern that consists of five separate candles, (see Fig. 5.5, opposite). The first candle is a white long day, and the following three candles are small bodied and usually confined to the trading range of the initial candle. These three central candles can be either black or white. It is the placement of these candles which implies a weak bearish downtrend, not their colour.

The final candle is also a long white candle that often opens at, or above, the opening price of the initial candle. It closes above the closing price of the initial candle, indicating a bullish perspective.

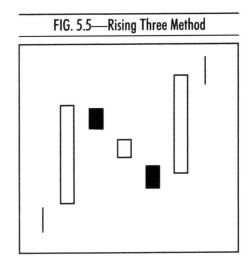

FIG. 5.5—Rising Three Method

If the second candle gaps upward from the initial candle, this pattern may be called a *mat-hold*. To avoid confusion, I will maintain the terminology of the rising three method, rather than seeking to define each variation individually.

Candle Addition

The rising three method reduces to a long white candle (see Fig. 5.6). This bullish reduction shows the power of the rising three method, and indicates that a less stringent form of confirmation is necessary.

Candle Location

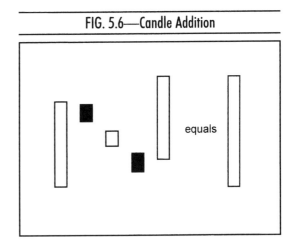

FIG. 5.6—Candle Addition

This pattern is found within an existing uptrend. Any subsequent candle with a trading range above the mid-point of the final white candle would be confirmation of a bullish continuation.

A common definition of an uptrend is for an instrument to consistently experience higher lows and higher highs. This pattern complies with this definition because the final candle displays a more bullish close than the initial candle.

Psychology

The rising three method does not occur frequently, but it offers a high probability of bullish trend continuation. The main reason that I have provided it for you to observe is due to the lessons that it teaches us regarding trader psychology. These lessons are important to understand in order to come to grips with the bullish or bearish tendencies of other candlesticks.

Occasionally you will notice a candlestick on a chart that defies any traditional definition, no matter how many candlestick books you look at. If you are in tune with the psychology behind the candlestick, you may be able to form your own conclusions about the nature of the new pattern. This is one of the reasons why the process of candle addition is so essential. It allows you to get in touch with the true meaning of new candle formations.

With the rising three method, you will notice that it takes three bearish sessions for the share price to drop in value to the opening price of the initial candle. In addition, this bearish effort to drive the price down was totally eradicated within the one final bullish session. The bearish sessions were lack lustre when compared to the decisive direction of the bullish white candles.

The number of sessions that it takes for a candle to reach a price level is very important for any form of multiple-line candlesticks.

In Fig. 5.7, it is apparent that Telstra 2 had experienced a period of sustained white candle uptrend, prior to the appearance of the rising three method. This continual white candle activity is unlikely to be sustained for more than eight or thirteen sessions according to candlestick philosophy. The bulls exhaust themselves, which paves the way for a bearish period of consolidation. The last long white candle that forms the rising three method is of significance. Note how this candle closed above the close of the initial candle. This is a sign of bullish continuation. (The last of the three black central candles that form this pattern has actually slipped below the open of the initial session, so this formation does not fulfil the perfect definition. This is an acceptable variation of this pattern.)

FIG. 5.7—Telstra 2 Daily

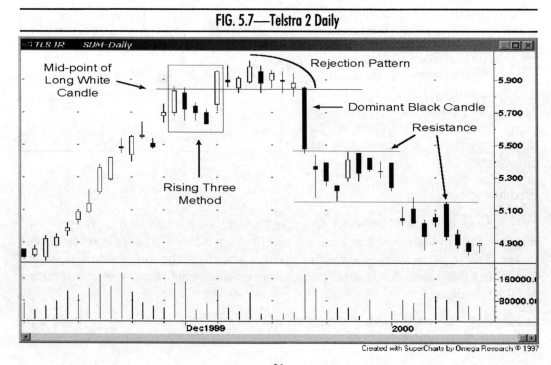

Created with SuperCharts by Omega Research ® 1997

Notice how the trading sessions following this final white candle have had trouble establishing a close below the mid-point? This may provide confirmation that the rising three method in this chart is likely to indicate bullish continuation of the existing trend. However, have a look at the long upper tails on the candlesticks that formed after the rising three method. This is a rejection pattern suggesting that the bullish upward movement was struggling. When a dominant black candle formed, notice how it began its life at the mid-point of the long white candle? This is very common behaviour. The mid-point and base of this dominant black candle can be expected to act as a future level of resistance. This can be clearly identified in Fig. 5.7. When a downward gap occurs in the chart, it can be expected that this gap will also act as a future level of resistance.

FALLING THREE METHOD

Description

This bearish continuation pattern is the equal, but opposite, counterpart to the rising three method. The first black long candle precedes three small-bodied candles. These three candles are mostly contained within the real body range of the initial candle and can be either black or white. It is the placement of these candles which implies a weak bullish uptrend, not their colour.

The final candle has a long black real body that closes below the body of the initial candle. This close at a lower price level ensures that the pattern has made a lower low, therefore it is undeniably bearish, (see Fig. 5.8).

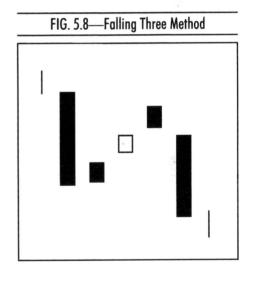

FIG. 5.8—Falling Three Method

A common definition of a downtrend is for an instrument to experience consistently lower highs and lower lows. This pattern complies with this definition.

Candle Addition

The falling three method reduces to one long black candle which fully supports the bearish continuation, (see Fig. 5.9, overleaf).

Candle Location

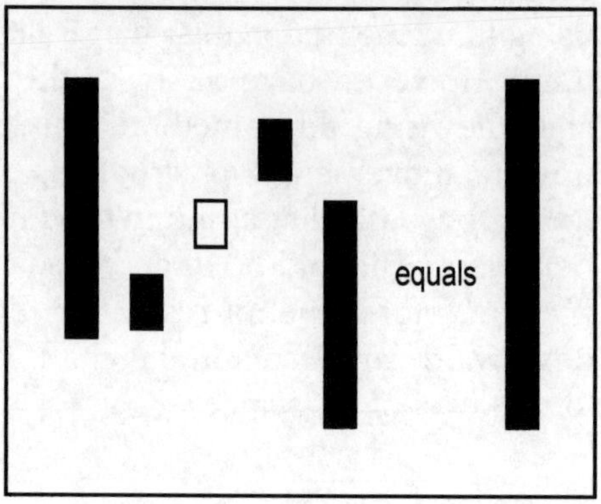

The share must be in a downtrend when the falling three method forms. If the session following the trigger closed below the mid-point of the final candle, it would be confirmed as bearish in nature, and it is highly likely that the downtrend would continue.

Psychology

The two strongest sessions in this pattern clearly have a bearish intent as is evident by their black long real bodies. The three small bodies at the centre do not have the same emotional intensity as the long bodies at the beginning and end of the formation. It took the share three sessions to move up to the opening price of the initial candle, yet this bullish behaviour was eradicated in only one session by the final candle.

FIG. 5.9—Candle Addition

equals

FINAL THOUGHTS ON CONTINUATION PATTERNS

You will find many other examples of continuation patterns in other alternative candlestick texts. For years I have sought to find clear, consistently occurring examples in Australian charts. Unfortunately, I have not been able to utilise these other continuation patterns in the same way that I have profitably traded with reversals.

Reversal patterns can be found easily and provide many examples of their effectiveness. Continuation patterns are far less common, and therefore I have not supplied an exhaustive list of rare examples. Perhaps you could allow the continuation patterns that we have discussed to confirm your knowledge about the psychology guiding the creation of the candle, rather than dismiss them altogether. The lessons that they can teach us are valuable, even if their appearance in Australian charts is infrequent.

REVIEW

1) Name the three components of making a trade.

2) Continuation patterns are largely useless in candlestick philosophy:

(a) True   (b) False

3) Explain the relevance of the number of bullish sessions compared to the number of bearish sessions that it takes for a share to reach a particular price. (Hint: Refer to the rising three method.)

_____

_____

ANSWERS

1) The three components of a trade are: opportunity identification, placing the order, and money and risk management.

2) (b) False. Even though there are few examples of traditional continuation patterns in Australian charts, the philosophy behind the formation of them is important to understand.

3) With the rising three method, you will notice that it takes three bearish sessions for the share price to drop in value to the opening price of the initial white candle. This bearish effort to drive the price down was totally eradicated within the one final bullish session. The bearish sessions did not display the same level of emotional conviction, in comparison to the bullish sessions. This assists in establishing which team is in control—the bulls or the bears.

➔ ➔ ➔   *Gaps will help you understand the true meaning of many candlestick patterns. Keep reading to find out how they can positively impact your trading...* ➔ ➔ ➔

PART II

ANALYSIS
SECRETS

Chapter 6

CANDLES AND GAPS

Gaps are often referred to as *windows* in candlestick terminology. 'Gaps' and 'windows' are completely interchangeable terms. They show that the price activity of the new candlestick is completely outside the preceding period. To fulfil the exact definition of a gap, even the shadows of the new candle must be completely outside the range of the previous candle. The effect is the creation of a 'hole' in the chart. A less stringent definition is to regard a gap as being between the real bodies of two candles. This is also a relevant and useful variation on the initial definition.

Generally, if a new candle has gapped upward from the previous trading activity, on significant relative volume levels, this is a bullish signal. The volume confirmation of an uptrending gap is much more significant than if an instrument gapped downwards. Shares can drop from great heights quite easily, almost as if gravity was pulling them back down to earth, without any change in volume whatsoever. For this reason, a volume confirmation is not as necessary for any downtrending behaviour. If volume *does* accompany a downtrending gap, then my bearishness intensifies, but this is not an essential quality to confirm that a downtrend may be underway. In Western analysis, this type of bullish or bearish gapping pattern is often described as a *continuation gap*.

Any reversal showing gapping activity before and after the trigger candle is considered very significant. The gapping behaviour prior to the trigger candle is likely to signify that the share's movement in one direction is becoming exhausted. For example, it is possible for a gap to display the last efforts of the exhausted bulls to drive up the price, just before the bears move in with strength. (This is a similar concept to an *exhaustion gap* in Western analysis.)

A gap after the trigger assists in the confirmation phase. (This is similar to a *breakaway gap* in Western analysis.) This gap runs counter to the prevailing trend, and will often signify the beginning of a new trend.

In candlestick terminology, windows can either be open or closed. If a window is open, then a gap has been formed in a chart. This gap is considered to be closed only if subsequent trading activity occurs within the span of this gap. This includes the placement of the shadows of any subsequent candles within the area of 'fresh air' created by the initial gap. If subsequent trading closes a gap, it ceases to continue its role as a future support or resistance level. This idea will be discussed further in the next chapter.

The word 'window' provides a colourful demonstration of the use of language intrinsic to candlestick terminology. It is used to describe scenarios in combination with other candlestick formations. For example, it would be difficult to believe that any positive outcome could eventuate if a shooting star was going to crash through your window! The descriptive visual allure of candles adds to their appeal as an analytical tool. However, I will continue to use the Western terminology throughout this text, as it is likely that you will find the word 'gap' to be more familiar than 'window'.

EXAMPLE

Have a look at Fig. 6.1 (opposite). This shows two significant bearish gaps between long black candles. A gap related to a long or dominant candle will always be more significant than if the gap was associated with a short day. It is also interesting to note that the other gap depicted resulted in the appearance of a doji day. This is a clear last effort by the bulls to drive the price up, which failed dismally. The gap up to the doji, and the gap after this trigger, shows that the uptick was exhausted, and unlikely to continue.

It is evident that gaps can have either bullish or bearish implications depending on the lead-up to the gap, and whether that gap is confirmed by subsequent trading activity. Always examine the trading context surrounding the gap prior to deciding whether it is likely to have a positive or negative effect on the share prices.

If a gap is present and a reversal pattern is not apparent, it is most likely that the trend will continue in that direction.

It is important to note that short days indicate indecision. A gap upward is more likely to result in a bullish thrust if a newly-created candle is a long day. Likewise, a gap downward is more likely to result in future bearish prices if the subsequent candle is long.

FIG. 6.1—NAB Daily

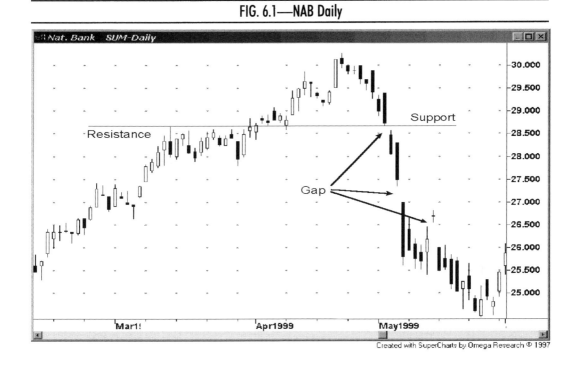

Created with SuperCharts by Omega Research ® 1997

GAPS AS SUPPORT

The study of support and resistance levels is essential in order to develop your skills as a trader. Support can be defined as a level where there is more demand from buyers than supply from sellers. This phenomenon creates a visible level on a share chart. You can actually draw a line through this level in order to watch for breaks in support. Any significant penetration of a support line can be assumed to have bearish connotations.

As with the upside tasuki gap, if an upward gap in a share is not closed fully by subsequent bearish trading activity, it is a sign that this gap may provide a level of support for the future. If a gap which should have served as support is closed, then my outlook is more likely to be bearish, rather than bullish. The actual support may occur at the top of the gap, at the mid-point or at the base. Support at the top of the gap during an uptrend would be the most bullish of each of these three scenarios.

A logical place to set a stop-loss for trading a share is just below the base of a significant gap. If the future share price activity

"If a gap is present and a reversal pattern is not apparent, it is most likely that the trend will continue in that direction."

breaks through a support gap, then your view should alter from bullish to bearish. This is especially relevant if the share *closes* at a lower price than the gap, rather than only experiencing an intra-day penetration.

GAPS AS RESISTANCE

Resistance can be defined as a relative upper level on a chart at which prices stall. The sellers want to exit the market and the buyers are reluctant to make a new high. At

> "Once a resistance level is exceeded dramatically, this often has a remarkably bullish effect on the share price."

that price level on a chart, demand has become thin. If this line is broken in an upward direction, this signifies that the bulls have managed to drive the price to a new level. It is especially relevant if a significant volume increase accompanies the breakout.

This concept forms a major component of my share trading strategy. Once a resistance level is exceeded dramatically, this often has a remarkably bullish effect on the share price.

It is interesting to note that gaps may often jump a significant resistance line to signify the continuation of an uptrend. If you do observe this, it is a very bullish phenomenon indeed. Let's review an example.

Have a look at Fig. 6.2 (opposite). The *tweezer top* (see page 103) displays two (or more) highs for separate sessions at the same price level. It displays a rejection of higher prices, and that selling pressure has now become evident. Notice how the gap totally jumped over this reversal pattern and that the next trading session created a long white bullish candle. The volume had also started to kick in, which confirms the bullish tendencies of this share at that time. Other traders must have started to sit up and take notice, otherwise volume would have been insignificant. Any share that ignores a bearish top reversal may be mustering the strength needed for a sustained trend upwards.

Often a gap which has formed in a downtrend will act as resistance on the ensuing upward push. In Fig. 6.3 (opposite) it is evident that the initial gap downward resulted in quite drastic bearish behaviour of the share. Interestingly, when the bulls drove the

> "Any share that ignores a bearish top reversal may be mustering the strength needed for a sustained trend upwards."

share price upward, it showed a real body hesitation at the level of the previous gap. Then, it actually hurdled that gap level and formed a white candle that acted as a continuation of the new uptrend. Notice the significant line of resistance that this gapping behaviour reinforces. It is very common to observe gaps that reinforce the existence of a support/resistance line.

FIG. 6.2—Techniche Daily

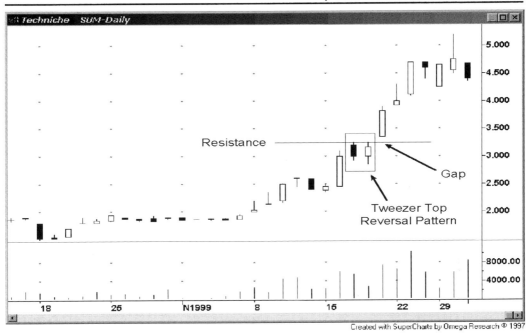

FIG. 6.3—News Corporation Daily

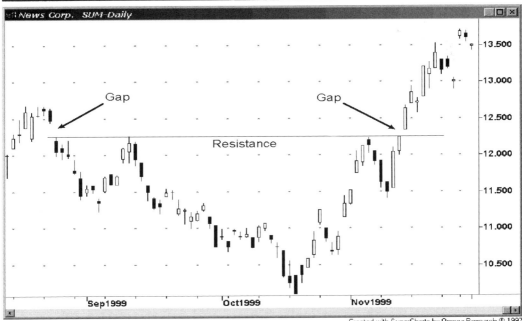

For traders who are short-selling the market, or buying puts in the options or warrants market, a logical place to set a stop-loss is at the top of, or just above, a significant resistance gap. If the future share price activity penetrates the top of a gap, then your view should alter from bearish to bullish. This is especially relevant if the share *closes* at a higher price than the gap, rather than experiencing an intra-session penetration.

TRAPS FOR NEW PLAYERS

Some gaps are not all that they appear to be! When a share goes ex-dividend, often a gap in the share chart will develop. A dividend is part of a company's net profit that is paid to shareholders as a cash reward for investing in the company's shares. This periodic profit payment to the shareholders is often made on a quarterly basis.

When the market is preparing for a dividend payment, the share price often increases. The market becomes enthusiastic about the promise of a dividend payment. Once a stock goes ex-dividend, the price of the share often falls dramatically. This share price drop will be immediate and forceful. In the majority of situations, a downward gap will be formed. An ex-dividend gap should not provide confirmation of the presence of any candlestick pattern. Believing that an ex-dividend gap represents a genuine change in price action is definitely not advised. Many ex-dividend gaps recover within five to seven sessions if the share is uptrending.

REVIEW

1) An upward trending gap requires confirmation via an increase in volume if it is to be considered a true change in share price behaviour:

(a) True   (b) False

2) An ex-dividend gap can be utilised to form part of a candlestick pattern:

(a) True   (b) False

3) Which of the following statements are true?

(a) Gaps are referred to as windows by traditional candlestick analysts.

(b) Gaps often represent a powerful move in market sentiment.

(c) Significant gaps form potential areas of support or resistance for subsequent trading sessions.

(d) If a gap is 'closed' by a candle, the power of that gap to act as support or resistance is lessened.

ANSWERS

1) (a) True. A volume increase is more important to confirm an uptrend than it is to confirm a downtrend.

2) (b) False. Any ex-dividend gap should not be utilised to form a candlestick pattern. A genuine gap may signify exhaustion of a trend, or a significant and powerful bullish or bearish change in market sentiment. An ex-dividend gap does not have the same implications.

3) All of these statements are true.

➜ ➜ ➜ _Just as gaps can form a powerful barrier of support or resistance in a chart, other candlestick patterns can have the same effect. The next chapter addresses some formations that have powerful significance..._ ➜ ➜ ➜

Chapter 7

SUPPORT AND RESISTANCE

Let's review the concept of trendlines, as well as support/resistance, and then have a look at some candlestick-specific implications.

TRENDLINES

A trendline is a useful tool to assist traders in determining whether a share is trending. An uptrend may be defined as a condition where prices consistently make higher lows. A trendline can be drawn on the chart to connect these low points, and when there is sustained movement below this line, the uptrend is likely to be broken. An estimation can be made regarding the strength of that trend by observing the angle of the trendline.

A 45-degree angle on an upward-sloping trendline is supposed to represent an enduring trend. This general dogma is paraded as a well-accepted truth. However, the angle of the trendline will be dependent on the scale used. Even an incredibly steep slope can be made to look like a gradual incline by expanding the date scale. A one-to-one scaling of your price and date data will ensure that a 45-degree angle of a trendline represents the ideal sustainable angle, but will often require hand plotting for all of your share charts. This is indeed a tedious step, especially when a computer can plot a chart complete with indicators in a millisecond. It is important to be aware, however, that unless you are using a standard one-to-one scaling for all of your charts, you will need to make a personal assessment regarding the angle of the incline that you find acceptable.

If the share is forming consistently higher highs *and* higher lows, a trend channel is formed. This is very bullish indeed.

A downtrend may be described as when a share consistently makes lower highs. A trendline can be drawn on the chart that connects the highest prices of a downtrend. This will result in a downward sloping line. Prices will often move in a sustained upward direction when this trendline is broken accompanied by good relative volume levels.

If the share forms lower highs *and* lower lows, a bearish downtrending channel is created. This characteristic represents quite a sustainable downtrend.

Other than these two conditions of uptrending and downtrending, the share may trade in a sideways lateral band for extended periods. Some analysts have suggested that this sideways movement can occur up to 70% of the time.

The unfortunate implication with a sideways moving share is that your capital is tied up, preventing participation in other more lucrative opportunities. This *opportunity cost* is a frustrating consequence of being involved in non-trending shares. Opportunity cost means that your money could be working harder for you elsewhere. The only method that I am aware of to make money out of non-trending shares is to implement an option writing strategy. (If you are interested in option strategies that will allow you to make a profit regardless of whether the share is in an uptrend, a downtrend or travelling in a sideways band, refer to my previous book entitled *The Secret of Writing Options.*) Generally, however, a clear trend in either direction is necessary to make substantial profits.

Diagonal support and resistance can be seen along a trendline. To avoid any confusion, though, I will refer to support and resistance lines as running horizontally. Have a look at Fig. 7.1 overleaf. This is a weekly chart that clearly shows some established support and resistance lines. (Note that for trading purposes, a closer examination of the daily chart after viewing the weekly chart is suggested. I usually start with a weekly chart and then review charts of increasingly smaller time increments for the share that I am interested in trading.) The support line can be seen along the base of a share's price action, and resistance can be seen along the top of a range of consolidation.

If the share has displayed an overall uptrending behaviour, a period of consolidation is very healthy. This pause allows the share to recover from its vigorous trading activity. I consider these ranges of consolidation to be like a tightly wound spring. This trading range, like the spring, often builds up a significant amount of potential energy. Once a release of this energy occurs, the bullish breakout can be sudden and explosive. Luckily, this allows us to recognise this change in behaviour and run with the bulls.

FIG. 7.1—ERG Weekly

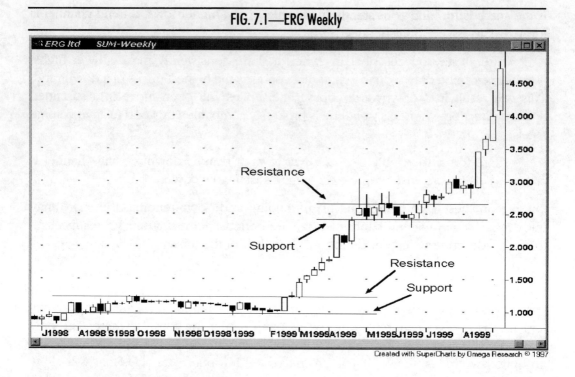

WHERE TO DRAW YOUR LINE

When beginners learn about the power of candlesticks, usually a question springs promptly to their minds: "Where do I draw in my trendlines, and support/resistance lines? Do I draw in a resistance line above the *shadows*, or above the *real bodies*?"

In my view, trend or support/resistance lines should be drawn at the level where the most points of the candles touch. For example, if the highs of several candles' *shadows* touched the $12.00 level, feel free to draw in a resistance line at that price. If there was a greater number of *real bodies* that would be connected by drawing in a straight line, then create a resistance line at this point.

Draw in trend or support/resistance lines at a logical price level that will benefit your analysis.

SUPPORT AND RESISTANCE CANDLES

Powerful reversal patterns can often be observed occurring at turning points of a trading channel, or at support/resistance lines. These patterns are likely to form a formidable barrier that future share price activity may have difficulty penetrating. This understanding will complement the strategies discussed in the next chapter.

A doji represents a very strong barrier to future bullish or bearish activity, so it is important to note the strength of this candle. Another point to consider is that the stronger the pattern produced by the process of candle addition, the stronger the level of resistance or support that it will create. For example, a bearish engulfing pattern will produce a stronger level of resistance than the dark cloud cover pattern. This is primarily due to the fact that the bearish engulfing pattern reduces to a black shooting star, whereas the dark cloud cover reduces to a white shooting star. As you will remember, a black shooting star has a greater bearish implication.

SOME NEW PATTERNS

There are a few formations that we have not yet discussed. These did not fit neatly into the one-, two- or three-line candlestick pattern chapters, so we will take the time to review them here. The following four patterns display rejection of price levels by touching that level with their shadows. All of the other multiple-line patterns discussed have been primarily evaluated on the strength of their body-to-body relationship. For this reason I have separated these patterns from the others that we have encountered so far. At the end of the chapter we will discuss dominant candles. These candles often act as powerful support or resistance to future market activity.

TWEEZER TOP

Description

This pattern displays the highs of two (or more) periods that form upper shadows with their peaks at exactly the same price. The candles can be of either colour. The upper shadows form a powerful pattern of rejection of higher prices. It is easy to see how this formation derived its name. It resembles the tips of a pair of tweezers (or more), (see Fig. 7.2).

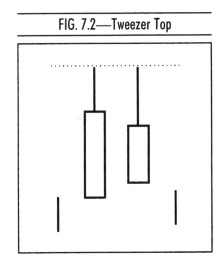

FIG. 7.2—Tweezer Top

If two non-consecutive candles form the basis for this pattern, I also consider this to be valid. Occasionally, the two peaks will be separated by several periods. This does not lessen the bearish implications. As long as the formation shows two symmetrical peaks with upper shadows at the same price level, it can be considered a tweezer top.

Some texts refer to a tweezer top as consisting of two candles only, and they do not take into account the appearance of tweezer tops with three candles. I believe that the greater the number of tweezers showing a reversal at the same price level, the stronger the implication. In addition, I have observed many examples of multiple tweezers in Australian charts. For this reason, I will continue my definition of tweezers as containing two *or more* candles.

Candle Addition

The candle colour is not relevant for this pattern. In addition, two or more candles can be included without affecting the stability of the signal. For this reason, the colour of

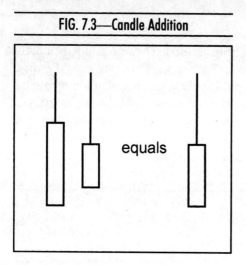

FIG. 7.3—Candle Addition

equals

the reduced candle created by candle addition is not relevant. This is also the case for the counterpart of this pattern, the tweezer bottom. All tweezer tops described fulfilling this definition reduce to form a single candle (of either colour) with a long upper shadow. This reinforces the bearish potential of the tweezer top, (see Fig. 7.3).

Candle Location

The tweezer top will be found at the top of uptrends, or within an uptick of an existing downtrend. Either location has a bearish implication. Even though this is a top reversal pattern, I have noticed that it can also be found within an existing downtrend where it will act as a bearish continuation formation. (My interpretation of the tweezer patterns as dual reversal and continuation patterns deviates from the standard definitions presented by other analysts.)

Confirmation will consist of a steady or dramatic decline in prices in the sessions after the appearance of the tweezer top. If the subsequent few sessions result in periods trading below the level of the real bodies related to the candles which formed the tweezer top, the inference is bearish.

Psychology

The price has tried to rally at least twice, yet has been unable to sustain this bullish push. Upper shadows were formed as a result. If the bulls had been successful, the tweezer top's upper shadows of rejection would never have formed. A white candle would take the place of the final candle(s), and the meaning would no longer be considered implicitly bearish.

When this pattern is observed as a top reversal, it represents a similar concept to the Western *double top*. The tweezer top *only* takes into account the upper shadows, whereas the Western version does not distinguish between the real bodies and the shadows. It also predominantly refers to a double top as being two roughly symmetrical, non-consecutive bars, at the same upper price, prior to a bearish

"It is a typical rejection pattern showing that the bulls are losing their dominant position."

decline. The candle's version tolerates the two sessions being side-by-side. The unsustained short-term price rally that creates the tweezer top is extremely relevant to candlestick analysis. For this reason, I believe that the tweezer top is a stronger indication of short-term bearishness than the double top. It is a typical rejection pattern showing that the bulls are losing their dominant position.

Until trading activity penetrates the resistance barrier created by this formation, I maintain a bearish stance, and my trading activity reflects this. Once the resistance line has been violated, my view is likely to become bullish. This line that acted as such a strong resistance will often then form support for future trading activity. This is especially relevant if the resistance was created over a long period of share price activity. The more touches of the high or close of a share price along a resistance line, the stronger the line. Traditional technical analysis dictates that three or more touches of the price along a trendline, or support/resistance line, are required for that line to be valid.

Have a look at Fig. 7.4. This shows a perfect tweezer top consisting of three candles. The greater the number of shadows, the greater the bearish influence on the share price. As you can see, once trading activity exceeded the price level of the triple tweezer, the bulls came out in force. Whether this rally is sustainable remains to be seen. Remember that the impact of a candlestick formation is only relevant for the next one to ten periods.

FIG. 7.4—Geo2 Daily

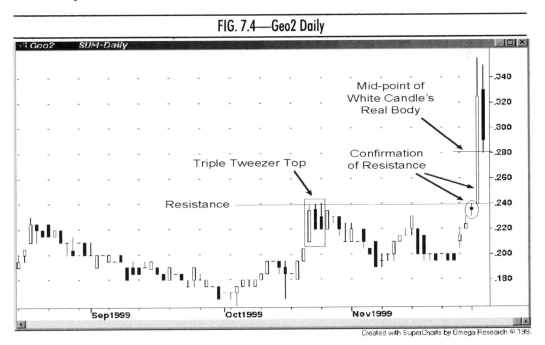

Created with SuperCharts by Omega Research © 199

When the tweezer top and spinning top was exceeded in this chart, then the result was undeniably bullish. A dominant white candle was formed with its opening price at 24¢ exactly. The significant increase in volume (not shown on the chart) ensures that this is a dominant candle, not just a long candle. This type of pattern showing an opening price at the exact level of the previous rejection is very common.

Once this bullish dominant white candle formed, it is relevant that the bearish final candle had trouble closing beneath the mid-point. This suggests that the mid-point of this dominant white candle may supply support for future trading activity. If there was a close below this mid-point, our short-term response may be to seek shelter, as the bears are likely to make an effort to establish dominance. A medium-term response may be to place a stop-loss under the *base* of the dominant candle in order to give the share a little more time to prove itself. The decision about where to place a stop-loss and the term of your view should be made prior to entering the trade.

Figure 7.5 also shows a similar pattern. The resistance line has been drawn at exactly $5.50. Notice that the breakout above the resistance level is violent and undeniable. The bulls have rushed in and produced a long white candle. This long candle is actually the dominant candle, as it was accompanied by high volume (which is not shown on Fig. 7.5). The upward gap from the point of breakout may supply some form of future support should the share price decrease (as discussed in the previous chapter).

FIG. 7.5—Gradipore Daily

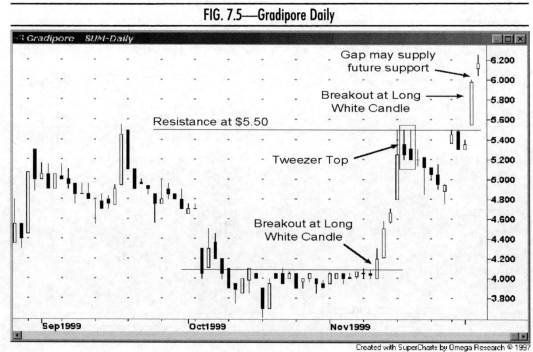

Created with SuperCharts by Omega Research ® 1997

A period of rejection or a reversal pattern after a significant breakout is common. In the Gradipore chart, a spinning top is formed after the appearance of this dominant white candle, and although this often signifies reversal, I suggest that you seek confirmation prior to acting in a bearish manner. The original shareholders often take between one and three periods to absorb this new information regarding share price and sell their shares at the level they believe is a good price. This is the psychology that creates a pattern of rejection or reversal. New buyers move in after a break of a resistance line, and it is the new traders' activity and excitement that drives the share prices skyward. This new activity may create a sustainable rally.

TWEEZER BOTTOM

The tweezer bottom shows the lower shadows of two or more candlesticks at the same price point before a rally. The lower prices have been tested, and rejected by the market. The colour of the bodies is not significant. The presence of multiple lower shadows creates the pattern. Higher prices are likely to follow, especially if volume is significant on the final candle(s) that form the tweezer bottom, (see Fig. 7.6).

FIG. 7.6—Tweezer Bottom

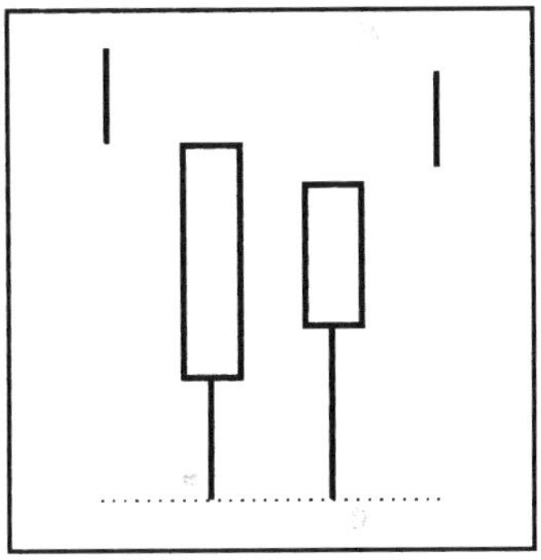

Candle Addition

This pattern reduces to a hammer. The colour is not important, but the presence of the long lower shadow of the hammer reinforces a bullish implication, (see Fig. 7.7).

Candle Location

This pattern appears at the bottom of downtrends. It can also be found within the downtick of an existing uptrend. In this situation, a tweezer bottom may demonstrate a pause in the uptrend before future bullish behaviour. (This definition, signifying continuation *or* reversal, deviates from some other analysts' interpretations.)

As with most bottom reversals, confirmation is essential to ensure that the bears are likely to give way to the bulls. Volume on the final candle is one such indication. A bullish signal is provided every time there are greater

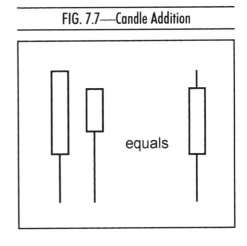

FIG. 7.7—Candle Addition

equals

volume levels on the uptick of prices, in comparison to the downtick. This is a general rule that holds true across any candlestick pattern.

Any trading which shows a bullish uptick will confirm that the tweezer bottom has performed its role successfully.

Psychology

Lower prices have been tested, and new buyers entered the market. Especially with the observation of heightened levels of volume, the implication is bullish. The bears were not strong enough to hold the prices down at the close of the final candle(s) to form a long black candle. The small intra-day rally that ensued formed lower shadows. This is a sign of bullish strength.

The tweezer top occurs more frequently than the tweezer bottom. It is important to understand the psychology, even if it may take you a while to recognise an effective example of these formations.

Figure 7.8 shows an example of a tweezer bottom on a chart. Remember to seek confirmation prior to acting on the basis of any candlestick, particularly a bottom reversal.

There are two patterns related to the tweezer top and the tweezer bottom. These are upthrusts and springs, which we will discuss next.

FIG. 7.8—IAMA Daily

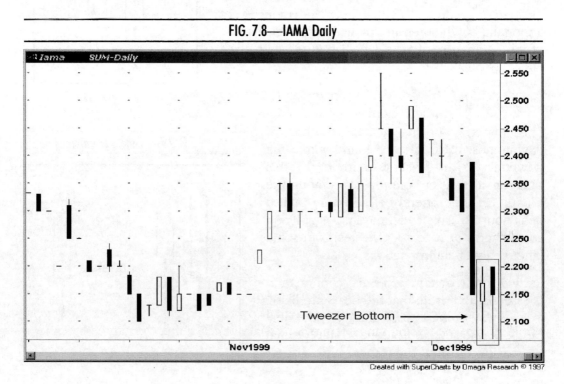

Created with SuperCharts by Omega Research © 1997

UPTHRUSTS

Description

The upthrust is related to the tweezer top. In this one-line candlestick, however, the *shadow* of one period penetrates a short-term resistance level dramatically prior to the share downtrending. This shows the final effort of the bulls to drive the share prices upward, before collapsing back into bearish dominance. Other related examples include a shooting star or a spinning top. The trigger candle can be either colour, however a black candle will

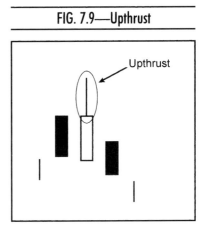

FIG. 7.9—Upthrust

Upthrust

be innately more bearish in nature. The long upper shadow must be above the range of the previous trading activity to fulfil the definition of an upthrust, (see Fig. 7.9).

Candle Addition

An upthrust can be formed by a single candle, or a group of candles creating resistance, prior to the appearance of a long upper shadow above this range. Therefore, the process of candle addition will reduce any of these patterns to a rejection formation showing a candle of either colour with a long tail. It will result in a pattern like that depicted in Fig. 7.3.

Candle Location

An upthrust is found at the top of uptrends, prior to prices experiencing a bearish decline. Confirmation consists of lower prices after the upthrust pattern. It is not necessary for a gap to be present before and after the trigger, as suggested with the shooting star or spinning top formations.

> "The long upper shadow must be above the range of the previous trading activity to fulfil the definition of an upthrust..."

Psychology

The bulls are showing signs of exhaustion. Their last effort to drive up the share price is quickly eradicated. This allows the bears to move in with force.

The upthrust has been provided to show you the signs of exhaustion of a trend, and the effect this can have on the share price. Any rejection pattern showing an upper shadow is intrinsically bearish. This pattern shows that if only the *upper shadow* is located above the trading range of previous share prices, rather than an entire candle range, it also has a bearish inference.

SPRINGS

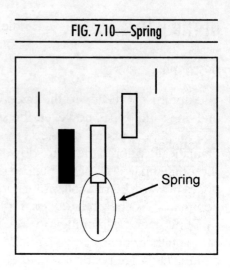

FIG. 7.10—Spring

Spring

Description

A spring is the bottom reversal counterpart to an upthrust. Prices test a lower price level and create a long lower shadow as buyers rush in and drive up the share price. The hammer is a related pattern. The spring will typically penetrate a lower price bracket than the levels of the most recent periods, prior to an uptrend developing. Although not necessary to define the spring, a white spring will have a more bullish implication, and a black spring will have a greater bearish impact, (see Fig. 7.10).

Candle Addition

A spring will form a long lower tail, which reinforces its bullish nature, (see Fig. 7.7).

Candle Location

Springs are found at the bottom of downtrends. The previous candle can be level with the real body of the trigger, so long as the long lower tail penetrates a previous level of short-term support. Upward movement of prices will confirm this pattern.

Psychology

As with the hammer, the bears failed to maintain a full downward movement for that period. If the bears had established control completely, this session would have shown a black candle with no lower shadow. The low prices advertised for buyers, and the buyers pushed the price upward.

DOMINANT CANDLES, MID-POINTS AND CHANGE OF POLARITY

Let's have a look at some other issues that will affect your trading results derived through using candlesticks.

THE DOMINANT WHITE CANDLE

Any long white candle with significant volume levels (relative to the previous levels of volume within the most recent trading periods) is considered to be dominant and has important implications. If a candle fitting this description breaks above a previous resistance level, its base or mid-point may become a key indication of future support levels.

The base of this candle will often be in line with the initial point of breakout, as it is in the Geo2 chart, (see Fig. 7.4, page 105). Another alternative is for a dominant white candle to have gapped up from a resistance line. This is common if an important announcement is released, and the market reacts with bullish enthusiasm, (see Fig. 7.11). An announcement regarding the ownership of this instrument was released prior to the start of morning trading, and this dominant candle was created.

FIG. 7.11—Bourse Data Daily

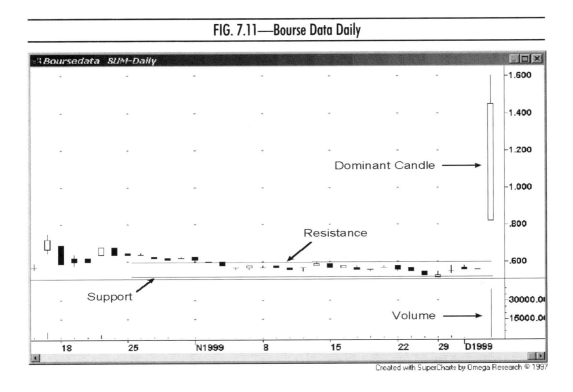

Created with SuperCharts by Omega Research © 1997

Either the base of the dominant white candle or the mid-point of the candle will often form a significant support level. This is of critical importance when establishing stop-loss procedures after a dramatic breakout. Conservative players could set a stop-loss at an end-of-day penetration of the mid-point of the dominant candle. More aggressive players may act on an intra-day penetration of the mid-point. Another alternative would be to await a penetration of the base of the dominant white candle.

THE DOMINANT BLACK CANDLE

The dominant black candle is of significance when seeking to exit long positions and enter short positions. This candle shows increased volume levels and a long, black real body. If a candle fitting this description breaks through a previously established level of support, this is of key significance. The bearish nature of this occurrence should not be disregarded. Dominant black candles often signify that a dramatic bearish foothold has been established. Volume is not necessary to confirm a downtrend, so if it is present, as it is in a dominant black candle, this is a particularly forbidding sign. This message sent by a dominant black candle is exceptionally strong.

It is so easy when we are in a long position to keep *hoping* that the share price will keep pushing upwards. The emotion of hope often blinds us to evidence that the instrument is unlikely to co-operate with our desires. The instrument simply doesn't know that you exist, so hoping that it will progress in a certain direction is futile!

As a trader, your views must be unhindered by emotion, otherwise you are very likely to suffer a devastating loss in the future. Rather than trying to convince yourself that the share is co-operating with your initial view, perhaps pretend that you do not actually own the share while performing your analysis. You should increase your levels of objectivity, or your bank balance will decrease accordingly.

"...increase your levels of objectivity, or your bank balance will decrease accordingly."

A dominant black candle dropping through a previously established support line is a signal that you cannot afford to ignore. Figure 7.12 (opposite) shows the consequences of maintaining a long view, even though the instrument has screamed at you that a short view would be more appropriate. If you listen to the candles, they will reveal their secrets to you. You just have to listen carefully.

Notice in Fig. 7.12 that after the black candle (1) drops through support, a substantial gap is formed. This gap is likely to form a barrier to future bullish share price action. In addition, the top of the dominant black candle after this gap (2) has also formed resistance. This candle is dominant because of the high relative volume levels associated with its formation (3). In order to establish a medium-term long view of the share, it is suggested that the share should rally above the top of the black candle, as well as close the gap by trending upwards.

In summary, the mid-point and top of a dominant black candle will often act as resistance to future bullish market activity. It is more bearish if the base of a dominant black candle acts as resistance. In the case of a dominant white candle, the mid-point and the base are likely to act as support for future bearish activity. If the top of the white candle acts as support, this is a very bullish sign.

FIG. 7.12—NAB Daily

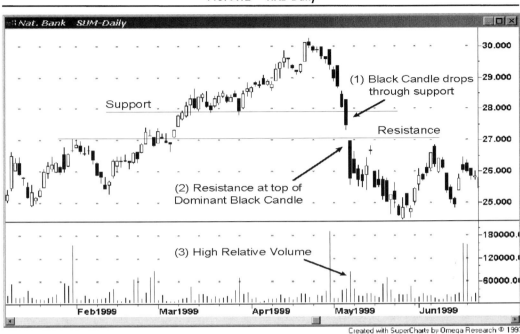

Nat. Bank   SUM-Daily

Support

(1) Black Candle drops
through support

Resistance

(2) Resistance at top of
Dominant Black Candle

(3) High Relative Volume

Feb1999   Mar1999   Apr1999   May1999   Jun1999

Created with SuperCharts by Omega Research ® 1997

THE IMPORTANCE OF THE MID-POINT

The mid-point of dominant and long candles often acts as a support/resistance level. This has been discussed at various stages throughout the book already, but it is worth making note of this observation here.

The mid-point of any long or dominant candle represents the shift in power from the bulls to the bears or vice versa. If the bulls are to establish control, they must make a visible and extended effort to show their power. If they fail to close above the mid-point of a long black day, then the bullish rally lacked power. The close of a subsequent session *above* the mid-point of a black day (by a white candle from below), e.g. a piercing pattern, is inherently more bullish than a close underneath the mid-point.

If the bears are to push down a share price, they must indisputably dominate the bulls. A meek growl will be insufficient to scare the bulls. If the bears manage to find a chink in the bulls' armour by closing below a significant mid-point of a long white candle, this is a critical sign. The bears have just won a battle, but confirmation is suggested before you jump to the conclusion that they have won the war.

CHANGE OF POLARITY

The change of polarity principle suggests that once prices break a significant resistance line, then this line will act as support for future trading activity. Also, once a line of support has been broken, it is likely that this line will act as resistance.

This observation will assist with your profit target analysis, confirming breakouts and pattern detection. It will show the points where the share price action is likely to hesitate in the future, and the location of a potential reversal, (see Fig. 7.13).

FIG. 7.13—CBA Daily

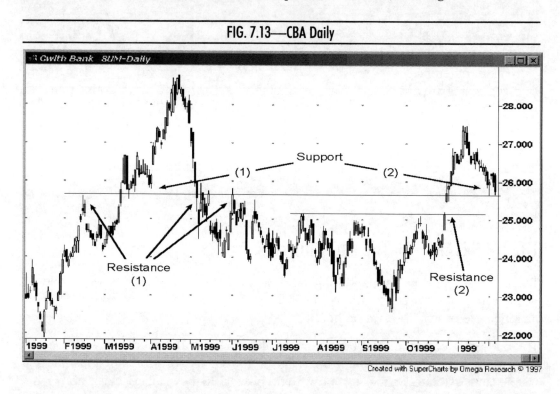

Created with SuperCharts by Omega Research © 1997

See, in Fig. 7.13, how the line which initially offered resistance (1), quickly became a level of support (1). A pattern of previous levels of resistance that become support lines is bullish in nature. At a later stage in the chart, resistance (2) was bullishly transcended by a gap. The top of this gap provides support (2) for future share price activity. This is also bullish. This level is likely to provide a springboard for future share price action. The confirmation that this is a valid line of support (due to the change in polarity) has established a foundation that is likely to reinforce bullish activity. If share price action was to tumble through that foundation, it is likely that this price level will once again become resistance.

PSYCHOLOGICALLY SIGNIFICANT NUMBERS

Levels of support and resistance are often visible at psychologically significant values. It is uncanny to see how many times a reversal in share price will occur at $2.00, $2.20 or $2.50 for example (see Fig. 7.5, with a resistance line at $5.50).

This idea of round numbers is entrenched in our society. Do you play golf? What happens at 8.00 a.m. on a fine weekend on any golf course in Australia? The course is flooded with people scrambling to get in first, isn't it? Yet at 7.50 a.m., the golf course is practically deserted! Play this trick of perception to your advantage.

It is *perception* that drives the market. When you buy a product for $23.99, why does this sound so much less expensive than if you bought the same product at $24.00? This minor difference in price is incredibly important to our subconscious (even though one cent coins are not available any more). Just as marketing managers make use of this information, you can use this same approach in your share trading.

Rather than selling your shares at $24.00, try placing your sell order at $23.99. I can bet you that there will be fewer sellers at this level, and buyers will react favourably, as they are likely to perceive that the price is closer to $23.00 than $24.00.

If you have a real-time data system that provides figures on market depth, you can observe this effect for yourself. Market depth shows a *bid* and an *ask* screen of the price level and volume of trades as they occur. Your broker has access to this type of information.

> "It is *perception* that drives the market."

I am constantly amazed at the number of sellers at round figures, in comparison to odd numbers. If you can make your offer more attractive perceptually to other buyers, then you have a higher probability of exiting the trade at that price. You may have to sacrifice a small amount of profit, but if you require your sell order to be filled within a set timeframe, this psychological trick may be just what you have been looking for.

REVIEW

1) Describe the change of polarity principle.

_____

_____

2) Draw a tweezer top pattern. Which is more common: a tweezer top, or a tweezer bottom?

_____

_____

3) What parts of a dominant white candle often act as support/resistance?

_____

_____

4) What parts of a dominant black candle often act as support/resistance?

_____

_____

ANSWERS

1) The change of polarity principle suggests that once prices break above a significant resistance line, then this line will act as support for future trading activity. Also, once a line of support has been broken in a downward direction, it is likely that this line will act as a future resistance level.

2) Refer to Fig. 7.2 on page 103 to view a tweezer top. A tweezer top is a more commonly occurring pattern than a tweezer bottom.

3) The mid-point and the base of a dominant white candle often act as support. If the top of a dominant white candle shows supportive tendencies, this is an even more bullish sign.

4) The mid-point and the top of a dominant black candle will often act as resistance. If the base of a dominant black candle is shown to act as resistance, this has a very bearish implication.

→ → → *Now that you have started to understand many of the principles related to candlesticks, let's see how we can combine this information with Western techniques...* → → →

Chapter 8

WESTERN TECHNIQUES AND CANDLES

One of the clients that I have trained in the art of candlestick pattern detection is a pilot. He often uses metaphors related to flying in order to describe the sharemarket. Specifically, he compares a night landing as being similar to trading. When you are 'flying by the instruments', you have to ignore any emotional bias that may take hold of you. Rather than trusting your perception that you are 100 metres in the air, it makes more sense to trust the instruments that suggest the ground is only 10 metres below. Without the discipline to follow this system with faith, it is unlikely that any pilot would ever land a plane safely at night.

Trading shares is very similar. If the weight of evidence of several indicators suggests that the share is downtrending, then the bears have probably taken control of the market. As with flying, it is possible for one indicator to be out of action, or for an indicator to produce a false signal. However, the probability of complete instrument failure is usually very low.

Personally, I would prefer the pilots on my next flight to have more than just one instrument at their disposal. Similarly, I suggest that you do not use candles in isolation.

"I suggest that you do not use candles in isolation."

Some candlestick enthusiasts are prepared to trust the candle alone, and never look at another indicator. I do not believe that this is the best strategy. By combining your knowledge of candlesticks with other indicators, a far greater depth of understanding can be achieved.

Many analysts add unnecessary confusion to the art of trading by analysing too many indicators. The addition of more indicators does not necessarily assist your trading efforts.

It is more likely to hinder effective trading habits. I suggest that you apply a weight of evidence principle to your trading. Find a maximum of four to six methods that you are happy with, and then look for each of these indicators to confirm your entry and/or exit procedure.

Martin Pring is a world-renowned trader, as well as the creator of many videos, educational CD tutorials and books. I personally derived a lot of benefit from his CD on candlesticks entitled *Martin Pring's Introduction to Candlestick Charting. Martin Pring's Introduction to Technical Analysis* is also a terrific educational tool, especially for the beginner trader. Pring lives in Florida, and I phoned him in order to gain an insight into his candlestick trading techniques. Pring stated that:

> In some instances a candlestick chart can be more revealing than a bar chart. I look at candlesticks when I find evidence that the market is about to turn. I mainly look at candlestick reversal patterns to confirm other indicators. Candlesticks come into their own when analysing the short-term trend. I use them as a supplementary indicator.

WESTERN TECHNIQUES

Let's review some Western techniques that may assist you in your analysis.

MOVING AVERAGES

A moving average takes the sum of the closing prices and averages them across a particular period. This indicator plots points which form a line when connected. A moving average line was designed to smooth out the fluctuations present when looking at the share price action. Instead of resembling the crazed undulations of a disco dancer, a moving average will make any share price action look like the movements of a waltz—steady, regular, and more predictable. They can also be applied to smooth out the gyrations of any indicator, such as a momentum indicator.

There are some basic principles that apply to using a moving average:

- Moving average lines that intersect have very important implications.
- A golden cross is where an indicator, moving average or share price crosses up through a moving average. This is a bullish sign.
- A dead cross is where an indicator, moving average or share price crosses down through a moving average. This is a bearish sign.

By combining this information with candlestick analysis, our decisions will be made based on more than just one indication of bearishness or bullishness. Figure 8.1 shows a daily chart of BHP. I use moving averages of differing timeframes in order to form my view on a share's likely direction.

In general, there are three types of moving averages—simple, weighted and exponential. I tend to use Exponential Moving Averages (EMAs). A full definition of this type of moving average can be found in the glossary.

FIG. 8.1—BHP Daily

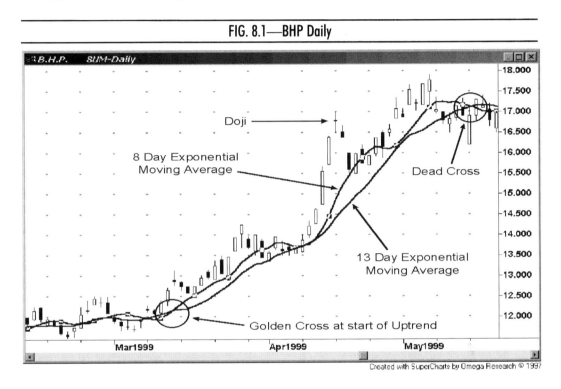

A golden cross of the 8-day and 13-day EMA is evident at the beginning of the trend in Fig. 8.1. A dead cross of the 8-day and 13-day EMA signifies a period where the share price started moving sideways. Between the golden cross and the dead cross depicted on this chart, there are several times that the moving averages touched, but did not fully cross. When analysing moving averages, I am looking for clear signs of crossovers, rather than acting when moving averages simply touch.

The appearance of a doji in Fig. 8.1 would usually signify that the bears are about to take hold of future price action. However, if we combine candlestick analysis with the interpretation of moving averages, we have not received confirmation that this is the case. The moving averages did not form a dead cross at this point. If we had acted based on the doji alone and exited our long positions, we would have missed out on the potential for a greater share price increase in the future. The doji only signified a likely short-term turning point. It should not be acted on alone if you are trading a

119

medium-term trend. Have a look at Fig. 8.2 to see the progression of BHP's share price after the appearance of the doji.

FIG. 8.2—BHP Daily

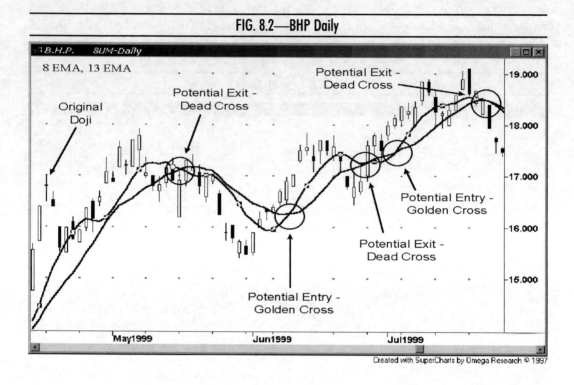

B.H.P.   SUM-Daily

8 EMA, 13 EMA

Original Doji

Potential Exit - Dead Cross

Potential Exit - Dead Cross

Potential Entry - Golden Cross

Potential Exit - Dead Cross

Potential Entry - Golden Cross

May1999   Jun1999   Jul1999

Created with SuperCharts by Omega Research © 1997

As you can see in Fig. 8.2, BHP eventually continued to trend upwards after the appearance of the doji. If you had taken the candle signal, you would have missed out on accumulating additional profit. Have a look at the entry and exit signals provided by the moving averages. I have purposefully used short-term EMAs, as candles are a short-term indicator. You will need to decide which timeframe you apply to your moving average analysis. By following the entry and exit signals provided by the golden and dead crosses, a far greater level of profit would have been achieved.

"Candlesticks are best used to complement Western techniques, not replace them entirely."

There is no 'magic number' to apply to a moving average, but in general it is suggested that you apply short-term moving averages if your view is short-term, medium-term moving averages if your view is medium-term, etc. Novice traders tend to develop an obsession with finding one indicator length that will be the answer to every trading situation in the universe. (Trust me—the search is futile. Even if a particular indicator has worked perfectly in the past, the changing nature of markets will ensure that this level of predictability is unlikely to be repeated in the future.)

Candlesticks are best used to complement Western techniques, not replace them entirely.

MOMENTUM

Momentum refers to the rate of change of a price trend. Indicators under this banner help traders to establish whether prices are increasing or declining at a faster or slower pace, (see Fig. 8.3). The Relative Strength Indicator (RSI), Rate of Change (ROC) and the Stochastic (STO) are all momentum indicators, and there are many more.

Some of these indicators have predetermined overbought and oversold lines. These are called indexed momentum indicators. These indicators have pre-set levels such as 20 and 80 on a scale of 0 to 100. For example, in relation to the stochastic indicator, 20 signifies an oversold condition and 80 represents an overbought condition. Other momentum indicators do not display these lines, but demand that the analyst make a decision based on whether the indicator has reached a historic high or a historic low.

These indicators are confusing to interpret initially, but here are a few simple rules that may assist you:

- When the indicator crosses down through an overbought line, this suggests that the uptrend is likely to reverse.
- When the indicator crosses up through an oversold line, this suggests that the downtrend is likely to reverse.
- If the indicator has been trending down and turns up, this is a buy signal.
- If the indicator has been trending up and turns down, this is a sell signal.

FIG. 8.3—Momentum Indicators

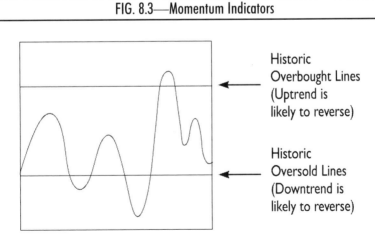

Historic
Overbought Lines
(Uptrend is
likely to reverse)

Historic
Oversold Lines
(Downtrend is
likely to reverse)

- The strength of the previous two points is intensified at historic highs for sell signals, and historic lows for buy signals.

- It is wise to watch for confirmation of these signals from actual changes in share price action.

Combining momentum with candlestick signals can provide valuable confirmation of potential turning points in the progression of a share's price. If you notice that a momentum indicator has reached an overbought level, as well as a candlestick top reversal appearing, then this adds strength to the argument that you should exit the share. If a momentum indicator is in oversold territory, and then a candlestick bottom reversal appears, this may trigger a buy response.

If you have two or more indicators confirming the strength of a potential entry or exit, then you are more likely to make a decision based on a very sound foundation. When several chart patterns and indicators point in the same direction, their signals are reinforced.

If you receive conflicting signals between any of your favourite indicators, wait for more confirmation prior to acting based on a candlestick reversal. By seeking consistency between all of your entry signals, you stack the odds in your favour.

CONSOLIDATION AND MOMENTUM INDICATORS

If a share has formed a base, or a range of consolidation, you will notice that momentum indicators will react in a peculiar manner. If the share breaks upward from the consolidation range, in all likelihood, the momentum indicator will automatically show signs of becoming overbought. This is because most momentum indicators are designed to register a change in the range of prices represented over the past several sessions. For this reason, the indicator will often be propelled upwards. Do not allow this to distract you. This will often signify the beginning of a new trend, or the continuation of the existing uptrend. Usually, I consider this propulsion into overbought territory after a range of consolidation to be a positive, bullish signal. This is a widely misunderstood fact regarding momentum indicators.

"I consider this propulsion into overbought territory after a range of consolidation to be a positive, bullish signal."

Turn your attention to Fig. 8.4 (opposite). This chart shows a consolidation range, prior to a breakout. The momentum indicator on the chart is an 8-day RSI. A novice analyst would perceive two conflicting signals, i.e. a breakout (a bullish sign) and an overbought momentum indicator (a bearish sign). However, if we alter our concept about momentum, we may conclude that an overbought momentum indicator confirms the range breakout.

FIG. 8.4—Energy Development Daily

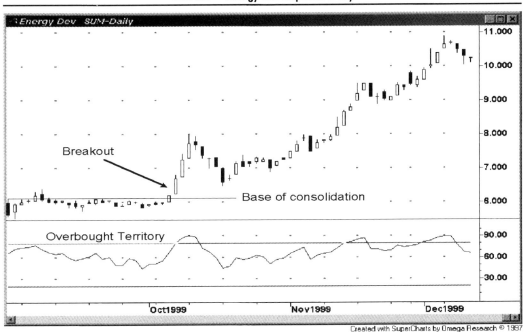

In addition, a favourable candlestick signal is also present. The candlestick pattern shows a gap upwards, then a strong white candle that definitively suggests the sideways trend is now over. There are three pieces of evidence conspiring to tell us the same story—enter the trade.

Another concept that you can combine with your study of momentum is to search for golden crosses with a moving average. By running a moving average over a momentum indicator, it is clear to see when the indicator is suggesting bullish behaviour. A golden cross of a momentum indicator with a moving average is bullish. A dead cross of a momentum indicator with a moving average is bearish. This concept will be explored further in the next section of this chapter.

THE SIROC

Often it is a challenge to find one charting software product to suit all of our trading needs. For example, some products are more appropriate for detailed statistical analysis, and others produce clearer graphics, etc. By changing packages to produce the next few figures (see Figs. 8.5 to 8.8), I am utilising the most appropriate software to illustrate several key points.

To create the next few charts, I have used a product called Market Master. This product is one of the few packages that will allow you to run a relative strength comparison (the next topic on our agenda). In addition, it contains a variety of indicators that are proprietary or unique to that particular software package. One of these indicators is the SIROC.

The Smoothed, Indexed Rate of Change (SIROC) indicator shows overbought levels (above 90) and oversold levels (below 10). Through its indexing and smoothing algorithm, it has a cyclical element to its movements. It can work well in both trending and range-trading markets. There is quite a lot of skill required to utilise this indicator to its full capacity. Rather than go into detail here, I have outlined a few general guidelines to follow:

- A golden cross of this indicator with a short-term moving average is bullish, whilst a dead cross is bearish.

- If the indicator is in overbought territory, this will be a bearish sign, unless there is share price activity above a range of consolidation. (As with most momentum indicators, this situation is likely to drive the indicator up into an overbought situation.)

There are several other guidelines required to fully interpret the SIROC, however these are the only ones that you need to be aware of in order to derive benefit from the discussion below.

RELATIVE STRENGTH COMPARISON

The Relative Strength Comparison (RSC) is a concept that is often confused with the Relative Strength Indicator (RSI). The RSI is a momentum indicator that conforms to the above discussion regarding overbought and oversold levels. Alternatively, the RSC is a rarely discussed method. This does not lessen its power.

The relative strength comparison takes the progression in price of one instrument and compares it to another. In *Technical Analysis Explained*, Martin Pring states that:

> Relative strength is a very important technical concept which measures the relationship between two financial series...Relative strength is therefore a very powerful concept for individual stock selection.

John J. Murphy states in *The Visual Investor* that:

> Relative strength is an extremely simple but powerful concept...savvy investors have learned to move money into hot sectors and out of those cooling off. In this constant search for tomorrow's leaders and laggards, relative strength is the driving force.

My own trading has certainly benefited from this concept.

A share may be trending upwards, but in comparison to the All Ordinaries Index, it may not have been performing as well as the other shares represented. This would suggest that a different share might represent a more appropriate instrument to purchase. However, if the share in question displayed a positive relative strength in comparison to the All Ordinaries Index, this would be a bullish sign. This share would have, in effect, been outperforming the index. I am aiming to identify shares that have been outperforming their sector, in sectors that have been outperforming the All Ordinaries Index. It is these little gems that I am seeking to isolate, and enter each trade based on a candlestick pattern and a favourable combination of other bullish indicators.

Gary Stone is the Director of ShareFinder Investment Services. He advocates the use of the relative strength comparison and has been a key promoter of this technique in Australia. In the next two sections, Gary explains how to use this type of analysis. He states that:

> The RSC is a tool that lends itself very well to using a computer to search for the high probability trades in a given market. Two methods can be used to achieve this—top down analysis and bottom up analysis.

TOP DOWN ANALYSIS

Top down analysis involves using the RSC to relatively compare each Sector Index with the overall market average, e.g. the All Ordinaries Index. This will lead the investor to the sectors that have the most positive market sentiment. Once these sectors have been identified, the next step is to find the stocks in those sectors that are outperforming their respective Sector Index. Using the RSC to compare each stock in the sector to its corresponding Sector Index does this.

To be carried out effectively, top down analysis requires the software to contain a database with a sequential listing of the Indices that represent the sectors of the market, and for all of the stocks in the market to be allocated to their respective sectors.

BOTTOM UP ANALYSIS

Bottom up analysis involves using the power of the computer to search for shares that are outperforming the All Ordinaries Index, regardless of which market sector they belong to. This list of shares can be viewed to seek entry signals using other technical indicators such as candlesticks, momentum indicators and volume.

Bottom up analysis requires a software product that has an "A to Z database".

Gary cautions that:

> As powerful as RSC analysis is, it will only identify which stocks to focus on, not when to enter. It should, therefore, always be used in conjunction with other indicators to determine when to enter the trade.

Some software products require a complete restructuring of the database to cater for the relative strength comparison analysis. Market Master is one of the only products that has its database structured in a way that allows for both a top down analysis and a bottom up analysis. These searches can be conducted quickly and effectively. Without this searching capability, you would be required to spend numerous tedious hours searching for high probability trades.

PUTTING IT ALL TOGETHER

In Fig. 8.5, several aspects regarding relative strength are apparent. When using a relative strength comparison, it is ideal to run a moving average over the indicator to identify turning points. The golden cross on the RSC portion of the chart signifies the period when the share began to outperform the All Ordinaries Index on a consistent basis. Notice how this golden cross coincides with a break above a significant resistance line on the chart? This adds to the weight of evidence that this is a genuine breakout.

FIG. 8.5—Securenet Weekly

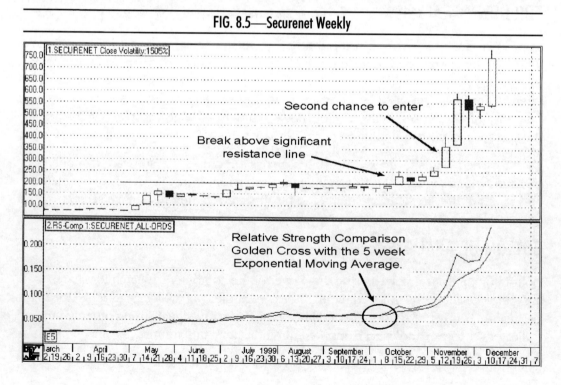

Even if you missed the initial entry signified by the break above resistance, there was a second chance to enter the trade as shown by either the pullback to the resistance/support line, or the long white candle. This long candle was a definite bullish indication.

Rather than just having only one factor leading you to believe that an occurrence is likely, it is more appropriate to wait for several confirming indications. What other indications would be necessary to suggest that Securenet in Fig. 8.5 was likely to rally? If the share price was positioned above its 30-week exponential moving average, perhaps this would add bullish confirmation. Another piece of evidence may involve a suitable momentum indicator creating a golden cross when combined with its moving average. A volume increase to confirm the breakout would also be of value, especially if the volume spikes (associated with the long white candles) were above the 5-week moving average of the volume. (Watching for a break of volume above a moving average helps to isolate the heavy volume sessions.) Figures 8.6, 8.7 and 8.8 show this combination of indicators.

Each of these indicators adds to the weight of evidence suggesting that the breakout of Securenet was likely to be genuine and sustainable. By seeking confirming indicators prior to acting, you will maximise your profitability.

FIG. 8.6—Securenet & the 30-Week Moving Average

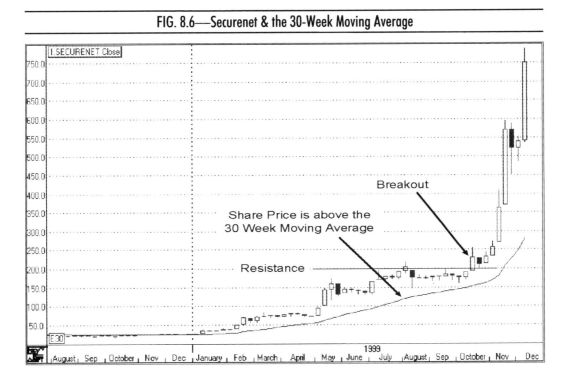

FIG. 8.7—Securenet & Momentum (the Smoothed Indexed Rate of Change)

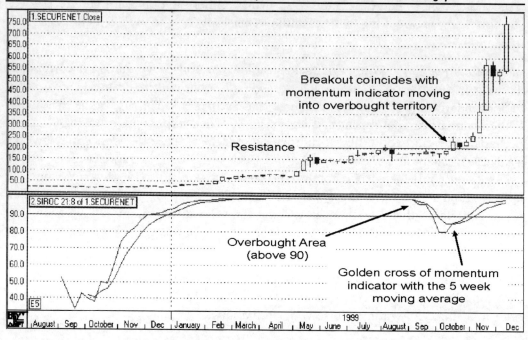

FIG. 8.8—Securenet & Volume

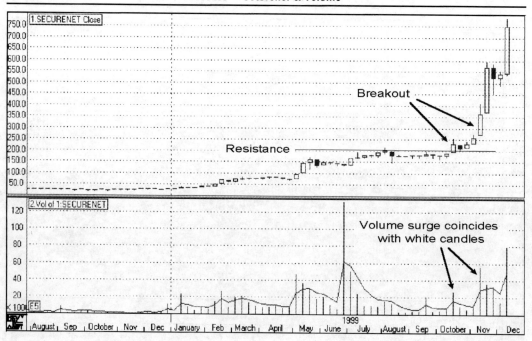

HOW I USE THE RELATIVE STRENGTH COMPARISON

Generally, when I am seeking to isolate a likely share candidate to purchase, I search for several confirming factors. A positive relative strength comparison of the sector with the All Ordinaries Index is initially important. Then I assess each share within these positively behaving sectors, in comparison to its other sector members. By performing this relative strength comparison, I am aiming to find a strongly performing share within a strongly performing sector. This process of relative strength comparison analysis assists in narrowing down the total number of shares that I have available for selection.

From this substantially reduced list, I look for several factors prior to making my purchase decision. A favourable momentum indicator, combined with an upward range breakout, on good relative volume, with an appropriate candlestick, will trigger my entry.

An alternative to this approach involves searching through all of the shares in the market, regardless of which sector they are in. Once I have found a share with a favourable combination of indicators and patterns, I always ensure that share has been outperforming the All Ordinaries Index prior to purchasing. Even if that sector has not been outperforming the All Ordinaries Index, it is essential that the share I have chosen to purchase compares favourably on a relative strength basis with the All Ordinaries Index.

Although I have several other methods of isolating high probability trading opportunities, I have found that these particular methods are extremely effective.

REVIEW

1) What is a relative strength comparison?

2) What are some key indicators that would provide you with a buying signal?

3) Overbought lines suggest that the uptrend is likely to reverse and oversold lines suggest that the downtrend is likely to reverse:

   a) True   b) False

4) What is 'weight of evidence'?

ANSWERS

1) A relative strength comparison shows how one asset is performing in relation to another. For example, if a sector is outperforming the All Ordinaries Index, that sector will display a positive relative strength. Ideally, you want to buy the strongest shares in the strongest sectors, and relative strength comparison will assist in isolating these shares.

2) The answer to this question will form the basis for your share entry rules. This is a personal decision. To assist, I have provided you with some guidelines about my entry signals in this chapter. Some of the key signals that I look for before entering a trade include a positive relative strength comparison of a sector with the All Ordinaries Index, and for strong shares within these positively performing sectors. These strong shares have several defining characteristics, including share prices above a 30-week exponential moving average, a golden cross of two exponential moving averages, an increase in volume on share price upticks, and a positive momentum indicator. The next chapter will add to this information and provide a framework for your share trading activity.

3) a) True. Momentum indicators refer to the rate of change of a price trend. Indicators under this banner help traders to establish whether prices are increasing or declining at a faster or slower pace.

4) Weight of evidence refers to examining several indicators to form a conclusion about the likely direction of the trend of a share. Rather than only referring to candlesticks as an indicator, it is suggested that you evaluate multiple indicators, prior to acting based on a particular formation. This is an essential process.

➔ ➔ ➔ *The next chapter will place your knowledge about technical analysis and candlesticks in perspective. A firm understanding about share stages will help you to recognise trades with a high probability of success...* ➔ ➔ ➔

Chapter 9
SHARE STAGES

A share can only display three types of behaviour. It can trend upwards, it can trend downwards, or it can range-trade in a sideways fashion. Given the limited number of options available for share price action, you may think that the odds of trading successfully would be very high. However, it is a fact that a vast percentage of traders lose money in the markets. If you examined the figures, it could scare you away from trading for life.

Only a persistent minority expend the necessary effort required to develop skill with trading. They are determined to play the game of trading and win, despite taking the occasional loss and having to confront their fear of failure. Those of us who are pig-headed enough to push forward and acquire the essential skills and psychological stability are the ones who will ultimately develop trading finesse. The fact that you are reading this book speaks volumes about your willingness to learn about the sharemarket. As a bonus for your persistence in developing the necessary skills to trade, I am about to share with you my breakout strategy. It is the primary way that I use candles to trade shares.

There are many alternative methods that I could have chosen to discuss with you, and I am sure that you will find your own techniques as you practise using candles. However, it is my aim to show you one of the simplest strategies to understand, as well as the method that I have found to be the most profitable.

Before we cut to the bottom line of my candle trading strategy, let's examine the likely stages that a share will often progress through. Skills of detecting whether a share is trending or consolidating constantly need to be polished. Conquer the basics of trading and the profits will follow as a by-product. An understanding of share stages will provide an overall framework for your trading activities.

STAGES

This next section is designed to provide you with the characteristics of each share stage, (see Fig. 9.1). I have identified likely candlesticks that may occur within each phase. By combining knowledge of the stages with candlestick identification, the reliability of formations can be more accurately assessed.

Not every share will conform exactly to the characteristics of each stage. Stage analysis is designed to provide a perspective on the likely progression of the price action, and it is not intended to replace the technical analysis skills that you have already gleaned. However, I have personally found that by analysing each share in light of these phases, my understanding about candlesticks has deepened.

FIG. 9.1—Crown Casino Weekly

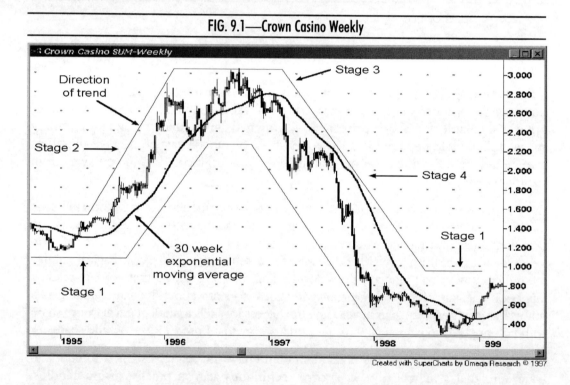

Created with SuperCharts by Omega Research © 1997

Stage 1

After a period of downtrending, a share will often form a base. This range-trading activity occurs predominantly between horizontal support and resistance lines. The share price is located mostly below the 30-week exponential moving average, and often candlestick reversals can be noticed occurring along the support line, and then the resistance line. This hammers out defined boundaries of share price action. (Note that I use the 30-week EMA as my standard for this type of stage analysis.)

The share is effectively treading water, and unless you have a short-term trading style, I suggest that you do not purchase a share displaying this type of behaviour. The share may consolidate, and trend downward from this stage. Alternatively, it may breakout and commence a new uptrend. I usually wait for a definite sign to act prior to entering a position.

The strength of the support or resistance line is intensified every time the share price reverses at that level. In general, a wide band of consolidation with significant volume levels forms a very strong range of trading in comparison to a narrow band with low volume levels. The heavy volume depicts that the bulls and bears are actively trying to assassinate each other. Generally, the higher the level of aggression by the players in the market, the more dramatic the breakout will be in either direction.

Towards the end of this phase, relative volume often begins to increase, even if the price action does not show bullish activity. Often volume will be one of the keys to detect when a share is accumulating the energy required to begin an uptrend.

Strategies to consider during this stage include writing call and put options. (Note that it is essential to close out on any threatened written calls close to the end of this stage.) Buying the share or buying an appropriate call option/warrant would also be appropriate if indications suggest that the share is moving into Stage 2.

Stage 2

In Stage 2 the share breaks above the resistance line established in Stage 1, and usually displays a decisive gap, or a dominant white candle on good relative volume levels. If volume does not accompany the breakout, this will indicate that the move is unlikely to be maintained. Notice how the share has broken above the 30-week moving average during the Stage 2 phase in Fig. 9.1? This also suggests that the rally is likely to continue.

After an initial rally, shares will often pullback to the point of breakout on low relative volume levels. The line that acted as resistance in Stage 1 has undergone a change of polarity, and will now act as a support level. If this level of support/resistance is penetrated from above, it is probable that the rally may not be sustainable. True breakouts rarely collapse back into the share price range established within Stage 1. If the prices bearishly penetrate the previous level of breakout, this will generally trigger my stop-loss, and I will exit the trade immediately.

In many cases, a candle reversal will be apparent at the base of this pullback (at the same level as the support/resistance level). Common candles at this point include piercing patterns and bullish engulfing patterns. This is a sign that the pullback is temporary, and these formations provide a second chance to enter a long trading position.

The less a share pulls back, the stronger the bullish impulse. If you wait for the pullback, you may miss an opportunity to enter a position.

Once the share has established an uptrend, several periods of consolidation will often be evident. New breakout opportunities can be identified during these periods. White candles outnumber the black candles during this stage, and the range of these bullish candles is often large.

The majority of my trades and pyramiding of existing trades will occur after the initial horse has bolted. However, the most lucrative trades are conducted at this first point of breakout. By keeping several shares that are in Stage 1 on a watch list, and being exceptionally attentive to any changes in share price and volume action, it is possible to enter the share either on the day of, or shortly after, the initial breakout.

The share is in uptrend during this phase and experiences a series of higher lows. Bottom reversal patterns during pullbacks are responded to with bullish enthusiasm. Top reversal formations have little impact on the bullish share price activity.

Be aware that the duration of this stage is not predictable. Take your cues from the share itself regarding how long the bulls will stay in power. Some shares stay within this stage for several years, others just a few days, especially if the breakout was weak.

This phase is of most interest to share traders and investors, call option/warrant buyers and put option writers.

Stage 3

The share forms a top, usually on heavy volume levels and exceptionally positive media reports. Many traders have made a lot of money during Stage 2, so the journalists tend to write glowing articles, extolling the virtues of this instrument. The buyers and sellers exchange many shares.

Towards the end of this sideways trending stage, the share price slips below the moving average. It is common to see the moving average line act as a resistance level. The bullish behaviour is running out of energy, so watch for a solid break below a significant support line. This support line break is especially dire if it commences with a strong black candle. Increased volume is not necessarily an indication that accompanies a drop below support. If the relative volume levels do increase, however, this may trigger a dramatic bearish descent into lower prices.

Be vigilant if you observe a top reversal signal during this time. As you will remember, top reversals usually provide some level of resistance for future share price activity, and bottom reversals provide support. In Stage 3, top reversals typically prove very difficult for the bulls to penetrate. In contrast, bottom reversals are easily defied by bearish activity, and do not result in significant rallies.

The ideal strategy during Stage 3 is to write a call option. If you decide to write put options, then take prompt defensive actions to close out these positions if the share shows signs of progressing to the next stage. Also, consider buying a put option/warrant or short-selling towards the end of this phase.

Stage 4

During Stage 4, the share trades below the moving average and experiences a series of lower highs. Black candles outnumber the white, and any level of support provided by a bottom reversal pattern is easily eradicated by bearish activity. The range of these black candles is often longer in relative terms than the black candles apparent in the previous stage. An uptick of the share price will often rise up to a previous level of support before continuing its downtrending activity. A top reversal pattern during this phase may provide an ideal opportunity to exit any long positions that you are holding. Often the moving average line will act as resistance.

Ideal strategies during this phase include buying put options/warrants, writing call options and short-selling shares.

SUMMARY

After a share has been trading in a sideways band for some time, it will often breakout and an uptrend will develop. This uptrend will eventually run out of momentum, and the share will again consolidate into sideways movement. This consolidation may give way to a break downwards, as the share price punctures a level of support. The downtrend will continue until the share consolidates again.

A 30-week exponential moving average can be utilised to identify turning points, and provide an indication regarding when a new share stage has begun. A firm knowledge about support and resistance and trendlines will also stand you in good stead to recognise these phases.

An understanding of these stages will place any candles strategy into context. For example, if a share is in Stage 1, there is a high probability that it will experience a rally and progress through to Stage 2. This progression from Stage 1 to Stage 2 is where I aim to implement a share entry breakout strategy. If the share is already in Stage 2, then I will look for a subsequent rally during the existing uptrend to either pyramid my original position or to make an initial entry. Another alternative is to await a bottom reversal during a Stage 2, as any pullback is likely to be temporary.

For more information regarding the share stages, I suggest that you refer to Stan Weinstein's _Secrets for Profiting in Bull and Bear Markets._

BREAKOUT STRATEGY

In this section of the text, I would like to focus on the breakout from a range of consolidation during Stage 2. This strategy will never allow you to pick the extreme lowest price on a share chart. Any traders who tell you that they consistently get in at the bottom and out at the top of a trend are likely to be misleading you (or suffering from an advanced case of self-delusion).

My goal as a share trader is to capitalise on the juicy middle chunk of the uptrend. To enter at the exact bottom of the trend and to exit at the exact high is an unrealistic expectation.

The system that I use to look for breakouts is devastatingly simple, yet incredibly effective.

In my breakout buying strategy, the major input into my purchase decision is price and volume action. This is the purest, most unadulterated form of available information. Indicators are, of course, interesting tools to use, but they are predominantly based on price and volume action. The raw data is very important. Candlesticks represent an alternative display of this raw data, so they are of paramount importance in my breakout strategy. In the context of share stages, candlesticks become even more powerful.

Volume is a signal of excitement or agitation. Bullish traders will display excitement as they seek to buy a share that will increase in value dramatically. Bearish traders will show agitation as the share drops in value. Their aim is to sell their shares as quickly as possible to preserve capital or profit. Both ends of this emotional scale deal with the human frailties of fear and greed tinged with a fair amount of desperation.

"Volume is a signal of excitement or agitation." For this next section of the book, let's assume that the share that you are aiming to purchase has fulfilled all of your other requirements as discussed in the previous chapter, e.g. a positive relative strength comparison, a favourable momentum indicator, share prices trading above the moving average, etc. We will focus on the specific candlesticks necessary to trigger an entry into a share.

OPPORTUNITY IDENTIFICATION

To identify potential share purchase candidates, I suggest that you search for shares that are trading within a consolidation range. There must be clearly defined levels of support and resistance. This will create the boundaries of the consolidation.

Consolidation can often be found at the bottom of a trend. Another alternative is for the consolidation to occur during a bullish run. This is a healthy sign as the share is pausing, prior to continuing its uptrend. The discussion below applies to both scenarios.

"...the overall trending behaviour of the share is likely to continue after a range of consolidation, unless the duration of the consolidation is quite long."

It is important to note that the overall trending behaviour of the share is likely to continue after a range of consolidation, unless the duration of the consolidation is quite long. This implies that a long period of range-trading is preferable after a sustained downtrend. If this is not present, then there is a strong probability that the share will consolidate briefly, prior to continuing its descent.

This also explains why only a brief period of range-trading is necessary prior to entering a share that is already trending upwards. The overall upward motion is unlikely to reverse if the range of consolidation is of a short duration.

Figure 9.2 shows the usual lead-up that catches my eye when I am searching for potential breakout candidates. If the share continues to trend in a sideways lateral band, I will not buy the share. I will await a breakout, and then purchase the share.

FIG. 9.2—WMC Weekly

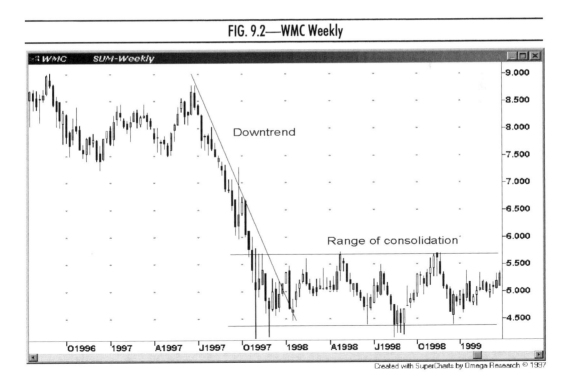

Created with SuperCharts by Omega Research © 1997

Generally, the longer the range of consolidation, the more significant the breakout, and the longer the ultimate uptrend. (There are of course numerous exceptions to this rule, but I have personally found it useful to establish some parameters of likely share behaviour prior to entering a trade.)

So when do I ring my broker, or feverishly type in my order over the Internet to purchase the share? Generally, I do not make a pre-emptive move, so I allow the actual breakout to occur prior to purchase. There is always a chance that a range of consolidation will only serve to continue the downtrend, so I wait for the share to tell me what its likely future movements will be.

> "...the longer the range of consolidation, the more significant the breakout, and the longer the ultimate uptrend."

By waiting for a breakout, rather than buying while the share is range-trading, there is a higher probability that the share will continue its bullish behaviour. There is a hidden opportunity cost of being trapped in a sideways trending share. All traders have a limited amount of capital (some more limited than others). Doesn't it make sense to capitalise on the areas where your resources will be working most effectively?

Figure 9.3 shows the breakout from the range-trading behaviour displayed by Western Mining.

FIG. 9.3—WMC Weekly

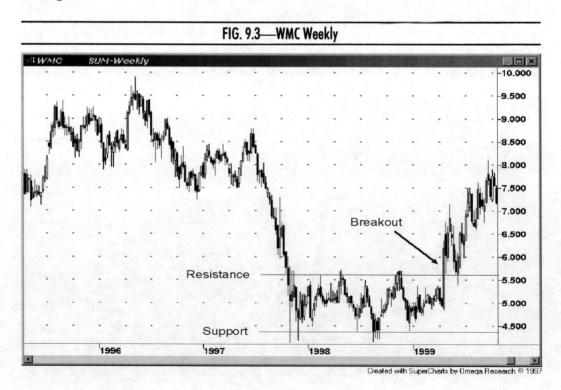

Created with SuperCharts by Omega Research © 1997

The term of your view will determine the amount of time that you are willing to allow your money to lie dormant and not experience capital growth. It will also determine the appropriate time increments for your chart. If your view is short-term, I suggest that you use a daily or intra-day chart. If you have a medium- to longer-term view, perhaps have a look at a weekly chart to form an overall picture of the share price action.

AN ALTERNATIVE PATTERN

Another pattern to seek, in comparison to a sideways consolidation band, is to look for a short-term, downtrending, range-trading share. This is a viable alternative to fulfil a breakout strategy. Figure 9.4 shows a weekly chart of Lend Lease. This share experienced classic signs of a downtrending channel within a long-term uptrend. Once the downward trendline is exceeded, this could be a trigger for entry.

Although many traders use this method, I have found that I am drawn to a breakout of a strong horizontal resistance line. You may prefer the break of a downtrend line. There is no particular method that is guaranteed to work in every situation. Often a fair degree of experimentation is required to see which type of trading style you will relate to.

FIG. 9.4—Lend Lease Weekly

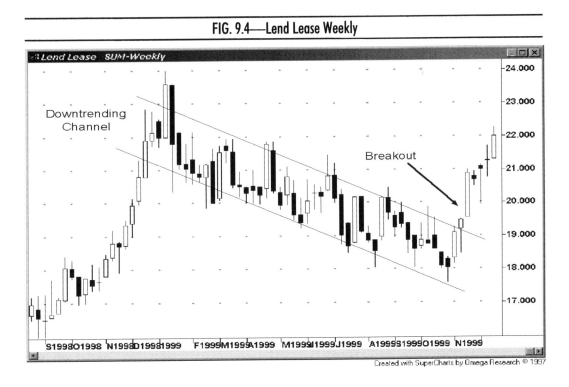

Created with SuperCharts by Omega Research © 1997

CHANGES IN BEHAVIOUR

Once you have found a number of shares trading within defined limits of support and resistance, watch for changes in behaviour. A change in volume may actually precede penetration of a resistance level. Volume increase shows that there is intense interest in the share, often from key players who have a vested interest in driving the share price up or down.

"I am keen to see a white candlestick push through a resistance line or minor downtrend line on heavy volume."

Obviously insider trading is illegal. It is definitely a practice that I do not condone (in case anyone from the Australian Securities and Investments Commission happens to be reading this). However, often the 'noise' of volume will be apparent before a significant share price move. This is an observable fact that exists in many shares prior to a significant uptrend. My observations are validated when the company in which I have just purchased shares using this method makes a major announcement to the media. (It brings me a perverse form of joy when the chart revealed its secrets without any apparent form of fundamental rationale at the time of purchase! This reinforces the benefits of allowing a share's chart to generate buy and sell signals, rather than tediously scanning newspapers or annual reports for hours on end.) I look for shares that display increased activity levels as this provides an indication that other traders also have heightened interest in that instrument.

I am most comfortable buying a share when there has been some level of confirmed movement in an upward direction. I am keen to see a white candlestick push through a resistance line or minor downtrend line on heavy volume. This is my ultimate goal in trading. To identify useful breakouts, there are several candlesticks that deserve vigilant attention.

PATTERNS THAT CONFIRM A BREAKOUT

Let's return to our Western Mining example. Generally, I suggest that you look for a decisive clear indication of a change of direction. The strongest and most powerful candle to indicate this level of bullish decisiveness is the dominant white candle. A volume increase with a decisive candle can leave you with no doubt regarding which team was in control for that session. It is a positive bullish sign if a dominant white candle breaks above a defined resistance or downtrend line, especially if there is little evidence of an upper shadow.

A gap upward from the level of resistance is also a clear sign that the bulls are about to make an impact. This is especially relevant on heavy volume, (see Fig. 9.5).

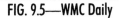

FIG. 9.5—WMC Daily

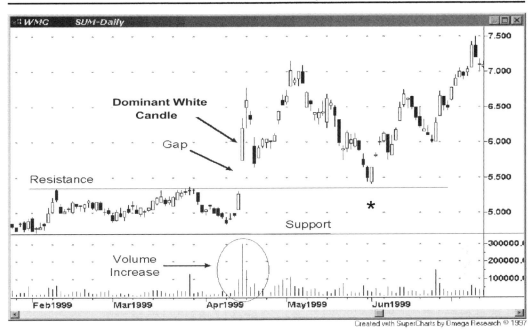

Created with SuperCharts by Omega Research © 1997

The chart shown in Fig. 9.5 is the daily chart of the breakout shown in Fig. 9.3. The actual breakout shows a gap upward, then a decisive dominant candle. It is dominant due to the relative length of the previous candles, as well as the significant volume increase present when the candle formed. In fact, the volume had been increasing from the end of the band of consolidation, which is a sign of bullish interest. Momentum was gathering, and the uptick was clear, visible and profitable.

Notice that the share price increased steadily in Fig. 9.5, prior to pulling back to the point of its initial breakout. This point is marked with an asterisk on the chart. Did you notice that there is a piercing pattern, which almost engulfs the black candle at this asterisk? As you know, this is a clear sign that the downward pullback has run out of momentum and that an uptrend is likely to follow. The piercing pattern was confirmed by the next session.

An initial breakout, followed by a pullback to the support/resistance line, is very common. The less a share pulls back, the stronger the likely future uptrend. This is why it is not wise to await the pullback prior to entry. If the share is especially bullish, it may never pullback, and you may miss your opportunity to enter.

It is ideal if this pullback occurs on low volume, and if the initial breakout occurs on heavy volume. This is very significant. A stop-loss should be set just below the point of initial breakout. If the share price plunges back to within the range of previous consolidation, the breakout is unlikely to be sustained.

ANOTHER CHANCE TO ENTER THE TRADE

If a share is already trending upwards, you could wait for a new breakout to occur. Alternatively, you could enter on a confirmed bottom reversal pattern during a pullback. If you are looking to purchase after a pullback, make sure that the uptrend line has not been violated. Otherwise, the uptrend may no longer be valid.

Both of these methods of identifying potential breakouts are key components of my trading regime. I suggest that you await the appropriate set-up to the potential trade, and ensure that each indicator (including candlesticks) has produced a favourable signal. This will maximise your chances of detecting trades with a high probability of success. By trading when all the lights are green, you will also minimise your brokerage costs. The other valid issues to consider, of course, are money and risk management, position sizing, and exit strategies.

There are many other tactics that you can implement with candles to light your way. Use your creativity. The strategies that you design for yourself are likely to suit your trading style more than a process out of a book. Have a think about how you can apply what you have learned in these pages to other share stages, and investigate different strategies to see which will suit your trading style.

SEARCHING PROCEDURES

It is likely that you will use some form of software package to assist searching for new trading opportunities. An automated searching routine will save you many hours of manual labour.

To automate your searching, you will need to input some guidelines into your charting package. One of the parameters that you could consider is for the share price to cross above its moving average. Once the share price breaks upward through its moving average, then you could visually check to see whether a resistance line has also been violated.

You could also seek to isolate shares on the basis of increased volume. Some packages will even allow you to search for new highs in share prices made over the previous two weeks, for example. There are a multitude of other approaches that you could use to search the market.

If you intend to maintain a short-term view, there are some systems that will allow you to register 'alarms' once a share has moved above a predetermined price level.

As an alternative, some brokers are willing to place a 'buy-stop', particularly in the futures market. This type of stop involves an immediate purchase of an instrument as soon as it goes above a set price. This is unfortunately not a common practice in equity markets.

I have organised for my mobile phone to alert me when the shares on my watch list have penetrated certain price levels, or changed in price by a set percentage. Perhaps you could ask whether your mobile phone service provider is capable of providing the same service. At the time of writing, Telstra and Optus have specific services available via mobile phones, related to the Australian sharemarket.

Paging systems are also available that display price, volume and chart activity. These useful tools may be worth a look if you are considering becoming a very active share trader. The flexibility of pagers and mobile phones has meant that traders no longer have to be screen-watchers to trade effectively. You need to decide the value you place on personal freedom. Personally, I prefer to invest in an effective service that provides me with the flexibility to leave the computer screen for the day without fear of suffering a substantial loss. Our success as traders depends, to a large degree, on the tools we use to conduct business.

Some software packages identify certain commonly occurring candlesticks. The SuperCharts package that I have used to create the majority of charts in this book has this capability, (see Fig. 9.6).

FIG. 9.6—All Ordinaries Index Daily

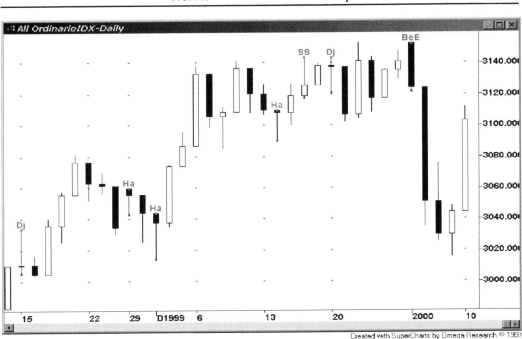

Created with SuperCharts by Omega Research © 1997

This is a terrific educational facility as you develop your skills with using candlesticks. The 'Help' function in this package allows for a written explanation of the identified patterns that will further enhance your burgeoning knowledge. The limitation of this function is that many of the computerised definitions of the patterns allow only for a very strict tolerance and do not permit any variation in interpretation. Once you absorb the meaning of each candle pattern, you will no longer require any computerised identification assistance.

REAL-TIME SYSTEMS

If your view is short-term in nature, it may be beneficial to investigate a real-time system, rather than using a standard software package that only shows end-of-day data. Be aware, however, that if you cannot trade profitably with an end-of-day system, it is unlikely that a real-time system will wave its magic wand and instantly convert you into a Cinderella (or Prince Charming, as the case may be) of the trading world. This is a mistake made by many novice traders. A shorter-term chart will not assist you if your trading methodology will not stand up to scrutiny.

It is important to remember that many traders confuse intra-day signals with a longer-term trend. In order to trade effectively, it is essential to examine a share chart using different time increments, such as weekly and daily, in addition to intra-day. Know your term before making an entry or exit decision. Match the session length on the chart to the expected term of your trade.

"Match the session length on the chart to the expected term of your trade."

Keep in mind that the intra-day time increment that you choose must be suited to the instrument that you are trading. If you are trading a highly volatile, liquid instrument in the futures market, a five-minute time duration for your candlestick chart may be appropriate. However, if the instrument you have chosen to trade is less liquid, then a one-hour chart may provide more meaningful results.

There are several systems available for you to investigate. Many of these systems seem to be priced for the institutional trader, rather than a private trader with budget constraints. Some systems require a dedicated on-line computer, while others access information via the Internet for an hourly fee. Do your homework before purchasing the first real-time system that you see. Make sure that you have located a system that is suited to your needs, or you may incur a substantial and unnecessary expense.

Given enough opportunities to practise your skills, you can become a successful trader. All you need to do is master the basics. For more information about how to use technical analysis skills that involve using formulas and indicators, as well as macro pattern analysis, refer to my book *Charting Secrets*.

REVIEW

Before completing this section, it may be beneficial to review the characteristics of each share stage in order to cement the concepts in your mind. With practice, you will be able to ascertain the likely share stage of any stock with lightning speed and precision.

1) Which stage is this share likely to be in (see Fig. 9.7)? Why do you believe it is in this stage?

_____

_____

FIG. 9.7—MIM Weekly

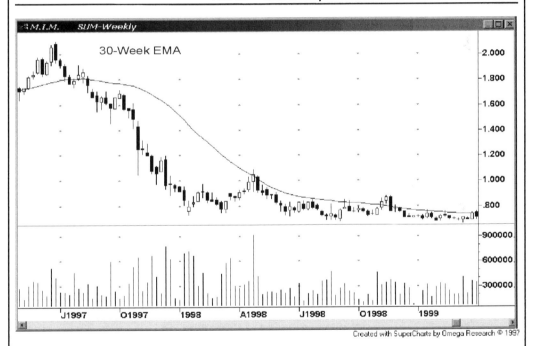

Created with SuperCharts by Omega Research © 1997

2) What indications would you be seeking to imply that the share had entered the next stage, (see Fig. 9.7)?

_____

_____

3) Figure 9.8 shows the share price activity in the weeks following Fig. 9.7 for MIM. What stage would you consider it to be in now and why?

_____

_____

FIG. 9.8—MIM Weekly

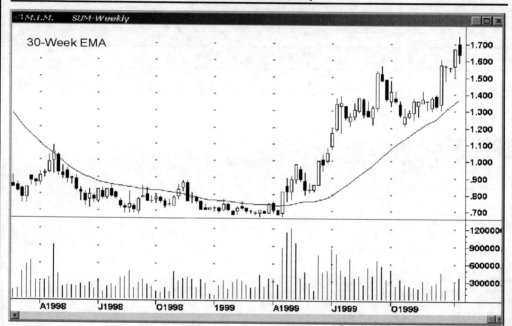

Created with SuperCharts by Omega Research © 1997

4) After analysing Fig. 9.8, what indications would you require to suggest that MIM was ready to move into the next share stage?

_____

_____

5) What types of strategies would be appropriate to implement during each share stage (buying the share, buying put options/warrants, etc.)?

Stage 1:

_____

_____

Stage 2:

_____

_____

Stage 3:

_____

_____

Stage 4:

_____

_____

ANSWERS

1) The share in Fig. 9.7 is likely to be in Stage 1. It has formed a base after several months of downtrending (i.e. Stage 4 behaviour). Prices are predominantly situated below the 30-week EMA (Exponential Moving Average) in Stage 4. The EMA is likely to show a sideways movement while the share is displaying Stage 1 basing behaviour.

2) Indications that MIM would be entering into Stage 2 would include a break above a significant resistance line on heavy volume, preferably initiated by a dominant white candle or a gap. When entering Stage 2, prices are typically propelled above the 30-week EMA.

A pullback after a significant upward price move is common. This pullback is usually to the previous level of resistance. The less a share pulls back, the stronger the upward move. A change of polarity often occurs, as this previous level of resistance becomes support. It is especially bullish if this pullback occurred on low volume levels. Figure 9.9 shows this pattern. If a share does not pullback, it may consolidate before continuing its bullish ascent.

FIG. 9.9—MIM Weekly

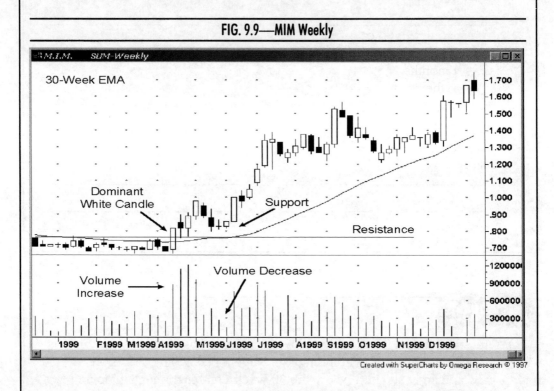

Created with SuperCharts by Omega Research © 1997

3) Figure 9.8 confirms that the share is firmly in Stage 2. There are some periods of consolidation, but the share shows a series of higher lows. The prices are positioned above the 30-week EMA. This is a bullish sign. It would be possible to draw a line connecting the lows. This implies an uptrend. If you missed the initial breakout, an alternative entry signal could be generated by a bottom reversal candlestick pattern positioned along the uptrend line. A new breakout above an established resistance line could also act as an entry signal.

4) Watch for signs that MIM is entering Stage 3. If the share price action consolidated for a significant period and prices began to dip below the 30-week EMA, this could suggest that MIM's bullish run was coming to an end. Watch for a significant break below an established support line with a long or dominant black candle. This downward movement is likely to signal an entry into Stage 4.

5) Strategies to implement while a share is trading in *Stage 1* include writing call and put options. (If a volume increase and/or upward price movement appears during this stage, it may be wise to promptly close out any of your written calls.) To purchase a share in this stage is not advisable, as the share could remain trading in this sideways pattern for several months. If you have received an indication that the share is likely to enter the next stage, then consider buying the instrument.

Stage 2 strategies involve writing put options, buying call options/warrants and buying the physical share. This is usually the lucrative stage that attracts many medium- and longer-term traders and investors. Ironically, often brokers are not recommending the share at the Stage 1 or 2 phase. It sometimes takes a while for the market dynamics to be clearly visible to all players.

Stage 3 shows the share forming a top consolidation pattern. Consider writing calls and puts. (Take prompt defensive action to close out any written puts if the share shows signs of entering into Stage 4.) Also, consider buying a put option/warrant or short-selling towards the end of this phase.

Stage 4 strategies include short-selling, buying put options/warrants, and writing calls.

By choosing the correct strategy, profits can be derived whether the share is in uptrend, downtrend or trading in a sideways band of consolidation.

➜ ➜ ➜ *So far, you have heard a lot about how I trade the markets. The next chapter includes an interview with a well-known character of the candlestick-trading world. Keep reading to discover the methods that David Chia, a Melbourne broker, uses to profitably trade using candles...* ➜ ➜ ➜

PART III

TRADING SECRETS

Chapter 10
A KINDRED SPIRIT

I am nervous. I am about to finally meet the man that I have heard so much about. Checked the make-up—I look fine. Adjusted the jacket, and now I'm ready. "I'm here to see David Chia," I say to the receptionist.

I am in the hallowed halls of a large Melbourne brokerage firm, designed to impress and perhaps intimidate. Chesterfield couches in the foyer, a huge arrangement of fresh flowers and a copy of the *Australian Financial Review* on the coffee table set the scene. The atmosphere reeks of success.

David bounds across the room, and greets me with a disarming smile and a warm handshake. He immediately puts me at ease. Not only does this man possess an extraordinary ability to read the market, but he also has a widespread reputation of caring for his clients, a rare commodity in the brokerage world. He is humble about his accomplishments and is always vigilant to keep any sign of 'pride' in check.

Trained as an accountant, and with a background trading every available instrument and market, Chia is now a dedicated technical analyst. He maintains a small, selective number of clients, hand-picked for their discipline and whether they are receptive to developing their skill as traders. Before you ask—David does not take on new clients. Believe me, he doesn't need to.

I was initially only going to provide a perspective on David's candlestick methods. As the series of interviews progressed, though, it became clear that this would do an injustice to the man. His candlestick methods are interwoven with his trading style.

Over several sessions, David shared his trading secrets with me…

How did you get started trading?

I am of Chinese descent, from a large family that was definitely not well off. I went to university in New Zealand and came to Australia because it offered more opportunities.

I've traded with several major brokerage firms for many years. The access to the information and the professional education that these brokerage firms provided was invaluable. Due to my accounting background, I originally traded only from a fundamental perspective. I believe that fundamentals drive the overall market, but it is the perception of people within the market that acts as a filter. Technical analysis allows me to analyse this filter.

I used to work with Chris Tate, and he originally introduced me to technical analysis. The way I viewed trading instantly changed. [Chris Tate is a mutual friend, trader, and author. Chris initially introduced me to David Chia.]

I read Stan Weinstein's *Secrets for Profiting in Bull and Bear Markets* and definitely related to his methods. I read everything I could get my hands on and I stumbled across candlesticks about five or six years ago. They've only been widely available in Australia since the early '90s. As soon as I understood the power of the candle, my insights into the market completely altered.

Do you trade for your clients only, or for yourself as well?

Unfortunately, I am bound by rules of conduct to trade only for my clients and not maintain a personal account. It is my role to empower my clients to follow the appropriate risk management procedures, and trade effectively. Money will be made as a by-product of following a good system.

If a client is not willing to set a stop-loss before placing an order, I suggest that they do not place the order—although the decision is ultimately theirs to make. There are some characteristics that great traders share, and a disciplined plan prior to entering a position is very important.

Many of my clients rely on me to watch the market and activate the buy and sell stops. That's why a lot of my clients stay with me. Several clients have been with me for years, and they have the skill to trade for themselves, independently. They don't really need me, but they stay with me.

As with many brokers, my first clients provided a valuable training ground. I honed my skills, and made a multitude of mistakes with their money. My current clients are reaping the benefits of my numerous early mistakes. I still make many mistakes in trading, and because I am advising clients, my mistakes are very public indeed.

What sort of mistakes do you make?

Usually I send out information to my clients containing analysis only, and not adding my opinion. I have come to realise that I am unduly influencing my clients' decision-making process whenever I add my own opinion. Who says that I know more than they do? It is my role to make them *aware* of patterns, and to empower *them* to make a decision.

A few weeks ago I sent out a message to my client base showing a candlestick chart of a share. I was so confident. I actually put five stars on it to draw their attention to what I believed was a 'sure thing'. As you could guess, the share proceeded to trend against my expectations—perhaps to teach me a lesson. Some of my clients have had emotional difficulty exiting that share because I made such a strong case to purchase only a few days prior. I could have kicked myself. You would think that I would realise by now that my role is to analyse, not to predict. Every time I pat myself on the back, I am really breaking my own arm.

Another mistake that I have made is when I have said to my clients that I feel that they can expect a return of 30% on a share. Where did I get that figure? I guessed. Some clients exit their positions once they achieve my fictional profit objective, only to subsequently see the share rise another 150%! Whenever I inject too much personal, emotive content, I influence decisions—to my clients' detriment.

I have even caught myself saying "I like this stock"! I cannot afford to 'like' any stock. There should be no emotional bias whatsoever.

Because all of my suggestions are documented, my humiliation is definitely public. It is far better when I comment on the formation, rather than seeking to overly influence my clients.

The times that I have suffered my biggest losses are when I have not adhered to my stops. Almost every time I make an exception, it makes an example of me! It has taken me years to learn that whenever I do not stick to my rules, I am likely to lose money. I continually strive to maintain emotional objectivity. I cannot afford to let my clients affect me emotionally, and I expect them to be disciplined even when facing a loss. There is one thing that I can state with clarity; I am definite that I have made more mistakes than the majority of traders.

How do you go about training your clients?

I hold group training sessions on several aspects of the market. They are open forum and very exciting. I have actually shed hundreds of clients to bring my client base down to a manageable level. I owe it to my existing clients to provide a good service, and I can't do that if I have too many.

I send out e-mails and faxes making suggestions regarding strategies, as well as entry and exit procedures. Most of these suggestions are candlesticks-oriented, but I also include an interpretation of other indicators such as moving averages.

Do you expect your clients to follow your suggestions implicitly, or can they have their own ideas?

Of course they can have their own ideas. Many of the shares that I become aware of are due to my clients locating them initially.

I aim to empower my people to become exceptional traders. They will never trade in exactly the same way as I do, but I know my methods work, so I do my best to make sure that my clients invest well. Some clients are day traders, some have a medium-term view and some a long-term perspective. In many situations, the distinctions are not always clear. Sometimes we find ourselves exiting prematurely on a short-term signal, even though we were initially entering with a medium-term indicator. This is one of the difficult parts of managing the trade with my clients—switching my mindset from one term to another.

> "The best traders approach the market as if it was a game, and really enjoy what they're doing."

I expect my clients to set clear objectives, and to express exactly what they want from the market. It is up to each client to keep track of his or her profit/loss situation. I won't do it for them. If my clients keep a record of their own progress, they are more likely to stay completely in touch with the areas that they need to focus on.

I tell my clients that I have a donut theory. The total donut represents all of the capital that we will keep from trading. I get to keep the middle part of the donut, and they keep the outside ring. As the donut grows, they benefit, and so do I.

What makes a successful trader?

Some of my most successful traders are women. It is my observation that they do not appear to be encumbered with as many negative male gender attributes such as ego, self-esteem, etc. They have the discipline required, and the drive, to achieve incredible profit objectives.

For a trader to do well, they must have passion and not just chase the almighty dollar. The best traders approach the market as if it was a game, and really enjoy what they're doing.

One of my traders has an expectancy of seven-to-one, and has made 85 trades this past year. [Expectancy is a better term than 'hit rate' for trading. It means that this client makes seven dollars for every one dollar that he loses. Seven-to-one is an excellent expectancy rate!] He gets 60% of his trades 'wrong' and quickly cuts his losses. The remaining 'winning' 40%, he rides until a change in trend. He actually loses on a greater number of trades than he wins on. You have to leave your ego at the door to do that.

Ed Seykota said, "The market always gives us what we want". I believe that this is completely accurate. Some traders will self-sabotage because they have personal issues that they haven't worked through. Their subconscious may ensure that they initially make a lot of money. Then they self-sabotage, and lose it all—time and time again.

I tell my traders that entry is only one issue. It's actually when you get out that determines your profit. Clients seem determined to tell me at what price they entered the trade. I am not interested because if they are in the trade already, it's when they get out that counts. The chart will tell you when to exit, not some predetermined set profit objective of 25%, for example. You ride the trend until the music stops for that share. Then you exit. The chart will guide your actions.

What limitations have you faced as your client base developed?

The main problem is the volume of shares that I trade for my clients. I can now, unfortunately, move the market if I send out an e-mail suggesting a 'buy' for a small or perhaps even a mid-cap stock. This is not a desirable situation to be in. I don't want to be the only one playing in a certain market. I have to make sure the *overall* volume of an instrument is sufficient, as well as the *relative* volume for that share. If the market makes a move, the relative volume must increase to support the direction of the uptick of the share.

Just before the 1994 correction, I sensed that something very bad was about to happen. The bond market tipped me off. I immediately sold two-thirds of my clients' holdings. Within a day the market nose-dived, and the screens were flooded with sellers. No buyers were interested. It took me an extra two months to sell my clients' remaining holdings. Once the market dries up, it is very tough to get out. When you see a signal, you have to act on it promptly and without hesitation.

For every time that I have correctly anticipated a market move, there have been dozens of times that I've been wrong. No trader will be correct 100% of the time. In fact, the majority of very successful traders only make correct calls about 50% of the time. There is definitely no room for ego in trading.

Why don't you trade futures and currencies anymore?

The toll on my personal life was too great. I'd be awake trading while my wife was asleep, then I'd go to the office and trade all day. Balance is very important.

[I laugh, and remind him that when he agreed to do the interview, he was actually at his office at 9.30 p.m. on a Sunday evening.]

Balance is still an area I am working on in my life. That is why it is better for me to have just a few clients to trade with. I can give more if I have fewer people, and if those people are highly skilled.

So tell me, I've always found candlestick reversal patterns to be more effective than continuation. How do you use continuation patterns?

Yes, I agree—reversal patterns are more prevalent and useful. I think continuation patterns are there to teach us lessons about trader psychology. They were never designed to be as powerful as reversals. The candle measures changes in buyer and seller psychology, and that is where they come into their own. They display a unique view of the collective psychology. I use all of the major reversal formations to a much greater degree than I do the continuation patterns.

How do you use candlesticks?

As with you, Louise, I am a great believer in the 'stages' of the share. Weinstein was pivotal in making this idea available to traders. Weinstein provided the framework in which to use candlesticks.

If I get a clear breakout above a downtrend line on good relative volume, or above resistance, I buy it. I keep hitting the trend by pyramiding my positions. This multiplies the profit. Because candlesticks are so visual, they assist me in making quick decisions.

I have always in the past leaned towards exiting a share completely rather than phasing out of a position. Because of the volume that I deal in now, I may pyramid out of a position if I get a trigger, and then remove myself entirely from a trade based on a defined time stop or a price stop. Once the share has gone past a strategic point, I exit quickly and completely.

It depends on the term of my clients' view regarding where we set the stop. The best traders always plan all aspects of their trade—entry, exit, and money management. It shows good discipline.

If the share is already trending upwards, then I'll buy on a bottom reversal, like a hammer. I'll pyramid into a trade using this method also. Sometimes I see the right candlestick pattern on an intra-day chart and I'll hit it at $2.60, $2.75 and $2.85 all within one day. That's a pretty short timeframe to pyramid. I take a lot of my signals from a daily chart, but without an intra-day candles signal I would miss the boat. I need the intra-day signal to fine-tune my entry. If I was using closing prices only, I'd never be able to get in early.

Sometimes I will make a pre-emptive move. We moved on Powertel the day before the breakout, [see Fig 2.12]. I'm not sure quite what told me to act, but I think you can take in a lot of variables on a subconscious level. Candles, technical indicators, market environment—when you've been trading for many years, you get a definite 'feel' for when a share is going to break. If you do the trade, and it doesn't co-operate, then you get out on your stop—no harm done.

Some inexperienced traders run into trouble if they say that they have got a 'gut feel' that the share will explode. My 'feel' for the market has been groomed over many years, and it is always based on a variety of indicators, not just a vague emotional decision to act.

If I've made up my mind I want in, then the intra-day chart will provide some vital clues. Look at this [he shows me an intra-day chart of RIO]. What can you see here?

I see a spring at the bottom of a consolidation range.

[David is truly delighted that I have identified a spring. He grabs my arm and says: "Now you're speaking my language!" I am secretly pleased. If there is anyone who I would like to impress on a 'candle-speak' level, it is David.]

That spring was the trigger. [He points to the real-time screen and I notice it is a 2-minute chart.] I'd already decided I was long in the share. We hit it once this trigger formed. We're still hitting it.

What time increment do you usually use for a candles chart?

It depends on the share. If there is good volume, and good volatility, then I'll use a tight session length. If the share is less active, then I may use a 2-hour chart, or just a daily chart. I do not make a decision made on a very tight timeframe. I only time my execution using this method.

If you had to start from scratch, what would you do?

Firstly, I'd get myself some excellent software, and a reliable data feed. The data that we receive as traders is the basis for all our trading decisions. Without effective systems, you cannot succeed as a trader.

The software would have to have a superior search engine, so I could look for changes in volume, share price, and other indicator values.

Then, I'd do what I do every day. I'd search the market, look for uptrends, pullbacks, and breakouts. To some extent, every time you look to enter a new trade, it's just like starting over. I have a clear idea of what I'm looking for prior to entering any position. I'll seldom act unless the set-up is ideal. Our business should be to react, not to forecast.

What do you do if you've missed the break [David asks me]?

If I miss the break, and the share has trended too far past its base, then I do not enter. I wait for a pullback.

Exactly—so do I. If the conditions are not perfect, you cannot act, because the risk/reward ratio has moved against you. That is why intra-day candles are so vital.

They provide an early signal to confirm the daily chart. Often a dramatic move will increase a share price by 20% in one day. If you miss this, it may be too late. The intra-day trigger is essential.

I have an 'elastic band theory' about shares. If a share has stretched too far past its base, it will often snap back down violently. That is why timing is important. You want to capture the main component of the move, and not execute too late.

[Our trading methods are uncannily similar! Both David and I are struck with this realisation. It is always amazing to find another trader who has independently travelled the same road, and reached the same conclusions about the market. Our systems have evolved separately, but we have developed many of the same triggers for entry and exit.]

After the interviews were complete, David sent me this e-mail:

> It was great to catch up today. It is not often I get a charge from another person in the markets. Your candour is refreshing and your passion and enthusiasm—an even rarer commodity. Never let anyone tell you it cannot be done—but I think you already know that.

I feel that I have found a kindred spirit in the market. David's energy and enthusiasm for his craft are apparent with every word. If you get the chance to see him present his strategies in a public forum, it will be an experience that will benefit your trading immeasurably.

One of the keys to David's success is that he has mastered his individual psychology. If you would like more information on this topic, you can listen to my *Psychology Secrets* CD program, available from www.tradingsecrets.com.au. In this CD, with the help of Chris Tate and Dr Harry Stanton, I explore the top ten trading blunders and how to overcome them.

To advance your skills with trading psychology even further, have a look at my *Trading Psychology Home Study Course*, also available via www.tradingsecrets.com.au.

Chapter 11

SEVEN GOLDEN CANDLESTICK RULES

It is time for you to be cast out amongst the other traders. The secret of the candlestick has been revealed to you, and you are ready to convert your new-found knowledge into money-making strategies.

Here are seven golden rules to assist you in your future candlestick trading endeavours.

1) Assess the Meaning Behind each Pattern

The candle graphically displays buyer and seller pressure. Candlesticks provide an insight into the collective mind-set of other traders. Rather than committing every signal in this book to memory, it would be far more effective to unravel the psychological principles that contributed to that candle's creation. Each pattern displays its secrets to the trained eye. With experience, your ability to draw conclusions based on candlestick formations will improve.

2) Analyse the Lead-up to the Trigger Candle

The lead-up to the trigger candle is equally as important as the pattern itself.

A share must be trending for a reversal formation to be effective. If the share is not trending, the reversal pattern will not have a significant influence. The only way to decipher the likely share price action after the reversal appears is to analyse the lead-up, and then look for confirmation.

3) Watch for Appropriate Confirmation

After the appearance of a trigger candlestick, it is essential to await confirmation prior to acting. To some extent, you will need to decide the amount of confirmation that you feel is appropriate based on the duration of your view, and your level of conservatism. Aggressive traders usually enforce a less stringent regime of confirmation prior to acting based on a candlestick pattern. Players who are more conservative may wait two or three periods. Confirmation is also suggested by using Western techniques, rather than relying on the candlestick in isolation.

4) Know the Term of Your View

Usually you can expect a candlestick formation to affect the trading activity of between one and ten subsequent periods. If you are a day-trader, you will need to be incredibly proactive if you are acting based on a daily chart alone. It may be worth your while to find a real-time candlestick supplier.

For traders with a medium-term view, candlesticks showing daily and weekly activity are usually sufficient. For longer-term players, a weekly chart showing candlesticks may be all that you require.

5) Do Not Use Candlesticks in Isolation

Despite the insights that candlesticks provide, I suggest that you do not use them in isolation.

No indicator will provide correct signals 100% of the time. Even if someone had found the perfect system, the market is based on so many variables that it is unlikely this method will continue to be effective ad infinitum.

Numerous methods result in an incredible success rate when dealing with the left-hand side of the chart. Unfortunately, we are not permitted to trade any trends that have occurred in the past. We must content ourselves with estimating future share price direction.

If we are relying on a system that is over-optimised, based on past data, clearly it will show incredible clarity when we back-test. Yes, it will be completely capable of detecting turning points in the past, but how will it perform in the future? This is called *postdictive error*. It is an unfortunate consequence encountered by many rigid, inflexible systems. Remain flexible, and allow your system for trading to evolve based on new market information, but do not use this premise as an excuse for not following a system at all. The best traders utilise systems in order to minimise the effects of emotion while experiencing periods of pressure.

Find just a few methods that you are comfortable with. Stick with those methods and give your system a chance to prove its worth before altering all of its inherent principles. If candlesticks are now included in your repertoire, this is terrific news, (I applaud your taste in indicators). However, if you do not relate to this method of analysis, there is no shame in that. Just find something that you do relate to, and use it consistently. If another method is more appropriate to your style, use it.

6) Apply Candle Addition to Multiple-Line Patterns

If you are unsure about the bullish or bearish nature of a new candlestick, apply the process of candle addition. This will assist in showing whether a multiple-line pattern is likely to have a positive or negative effect on share prices. By reducing several candles to one line, the veil of confusion is often lifted.

When you become fluent in 'candle-speak', you will be able to perform candle addition and candle development with speed and clarity. It is a skill that you will find very useful to develop if you intend to become proficient in candlestick analysis.

7) Back-test, Back-test and Back-test

Each share has its own personality. The way a share responds to different candlesticks is fascinating. Once you attune your eye to patterns within a share chart, many revelations will become apparent. Some are very responsive to certain candlestick patterns. This observation will assist in future trading scenarios, and may lead to a higher probability trade based on a new appearance of the same pattern.

For each instrument, look for the *frequency* of pattern occurrence, the *immediate responsiveness* to individual patterns, and the longer-term *effectiveness* of these formations. This process will provide some guidelines regarding how that share is likely to act in the future when a similar signal is exhibited.

It makes sense to focus on a few shares, and develop expertise in these instruments. This will assist in your detection of appropriate patterns within these charts. If you spread your resources too thinly by actively trading a multitude of shares in the market, it is possible that you will miss valuable signals.

Sun Tzu was a military genius who wrote a classic treatise entitled *The Art of War*. The principles in this ancient text are relevant whether you are planning a military coup, aiming for success in the boardroom, or desire to excel as a trader. The fact that his ideas were expressed approximately 2500 years ago shows that these concepts have stood the test of time. One of his adages is:

> If you know yourself and your enemy, you will not fear battle. If you know yourself, but not your enemy, you will lose a battle for every one that you win; and if you do not know yourself and do not know your enemy, you will never see victory.

This is exceptionally relevant for traders. I hope that the candlestick methods that I have shared with you have provided an insight into your own thought processes while trading. This is just as essential as having an understanding of the other players in the market and of market dynamics.

Congratulations on taking the time to investigate the lucrative world of the candle. I hope that you will enjoy using this unique tool and that your profitability increases as a direct result.

For more information about how you can combine candlesticks with other methods of trading the sharemarket, you can refer to my books *Trading Secrets* and *Charting Secrets*. To take your trading to the next level, have a look at my *Candlestick Charting Home Study Course, The Secret of Candlestick Charting Video Program* (on DVD) and listen to my triple CD sets *Share Trading 101—A Complete Guide to Successful Trading* and *Leverage 101—Maximise Your Returns,* available through www.tradingsecrets.com.au.

Happy trading!

FURTHER EDUCATION

Bedford, Louise, *Charting Secrets,* Wrightbooks, 2004.

Bedford, Louise, *The Secret of Candlestick Charting* Poster, via www.tradingsecrets.com.au.

Bedford, Louise, *The Secret of Candlestick Charting* Video Program, available on DVD and video via www.tradingsecrets.com.au.

Bedford, Louise, *The Secret of Pattern Detection* Poster, via www.tradingsecrets.com.au.

Bedford, Louise, *The Secret of Writing Options*, Wrightbooks, 1999.

Bedford, Louise, *Trading Secrets*, 2nd edition, Wrightbooks, 2001.

Bedford, Louise; Tate, Chris, *Leverage 101—Maximise Your Returns*, triple CD, via www.tradingsecrets.com.au.

Bedford, Louise; Tate, Chris, *Share Trading 101—A Complete Guide to Successful Trading*, triple CD, via www.tradingsecrets.com.au.

Bedford, Louise; Tate, Chris; Wilson, Matthew, *Power Trading—Trade CFDs Like a Professional*, double CD, via www.tradingsecrets.com.au.

Bedford, Louise; Tate, Chris; & Dr Stanton, Harry, *Psychology Secrets—Peak Performance for Traders,* double CD, via www.tradingsecrets.com.au.

Morris, Gregory L., *Candlestick Charting Explained*, McGraw-Hill, 1995.

Nison, Steve, *Beyond Candlesticks*, Wiley, 1994.

Nison, Steve, *Japanese Candlestick Charting Techniques*, Wiley, 1991.

Stanton, Dr Harry E. *Let the Trade Wins Flow*, copyright Dr H.E. Stanton, 1997.

Tate, Chris, *The Art of Trading,* 2nd edition, Wrightbooks, 2001.

Tharp, Van K., *Trading Your Way to Financial Freedom*, McGraw-Hill, 1999.

Weinstein, Stan, *Secrets for Profiting in Bull and Bear Markets*, Irwin Professional Publishing, 1988.

GLOSSARY

Back-Test: A method of testing an indicator's performance by applying it to historical data.

Bar Chart: This is the standard form of chart utilised in Western technical analysis. A single bar consists of an open price, a high, a low and a close price for a particular session.

Bear/Bearish: A trader with a negative expectation of the market or for a particular share.

Black Candle: A bearish session showing the close lower than the opening price.

Breakaway Gap: See *gaps*.

Bull/Bullish: A trader with a positive expectation that prices will rise in the market or for a particular share.

Call Option: A call option gives the buyer the right, but not the obligation, to buy a given security at a particular price up to and including the day of expiry.

Candle Addition: This process adds the candles of several sessions together to create just one candle. In effect, it takes the data from several periods and reduces it to one session.

Candle Body Size: The size of the real body can provide a clue as to the level of conviction of either the bulls or the bears. The presence of a long candle in relation to the most recent candles of previous sessions holds special significance.

Candle Development: Candle development dissects one candle to create many candles (of shorter time durations than the original).

Candle Range: The range from the high to the low, or the peak of the upper shadow to the base of the lower shadow, is a general indicator of the level of volatility for that period.

Candlesticks: A 17th century Japanese technique that uses the same information as contained in a Western bar chart, but provides a different graphical representation. Candlestick patterns of one, two, three or more candles (bars) provide an excellent timing/confirmation tool when used in conjunction with other indicators.

Confirmation: The activity of the share price action after the appearance of a *trigger* candle. Some candlestick patterns require greater levels of confirmation than others.

Consolidation: See *sideways trend.*

Continuation Gap: See *gaps.*

Continuation Pattern: After the appearance of this pattern, a share is likely to continue in the direction of the predominant, established trend. These patterns imply a pause or consolidation within the prevailing trend.

Correction: A movement against the trend that typically occurs with little or no warning. For example, the market periodically loses value as many of the underlying securities drop in price by several per cent.

Derivatives: A derivative is a financial instrument that has another asset as its underlying base.

Dividend: This periodic payment is a part of a company's net profit that is paid to shareholders as a cash reward for investing in the company's shares.

Dominant Candle: A candle showing a larger real body range on the chart compared to other candles, as well as significant relative volume levels in relation to recent previous sessions.

Double Top: This pattern is where price action on a chart displays that the price has rallied twice in quick succession and stopped at or near the same high. This pattern forms two prominent peaks in the share price action and often signifies that a downtrend is imminent.

Downtick: Any downward movement in price action. This downward movement can even be by the smallest available price increment available on the price scale, e.g. one cent.

Downtrend: Prices are making consistently lower highs and lower lows.

Downtrend Line: A straight line is drawn in at a downward right slanting angle, connecting the peaks of the share price action. Once prices show evidence of rising above this line in a sustainable manner, it is likely that the downtrend has been broken. Ideally, this should be accompanied by a simultaneous increase in volume.

Ex-Dividend: The day after the dividend has been taken by the shareholders. This typically results in a share price drop.

Exchange-Traded Options: The options traded over shares in Australia are called 'exchange-traded options' or 'American options'. This type of option allows the option holder to exercise the option at any time during the life of the contract.

Exhaustion Gap: See *gaps*.

Exponential Moving Average (EMA): The exponential moving average places more emphasis (on an exponential basis) on the most recent sessions and forms a moving average line. A moving average takes the closes of several periods and plots a point. When several of these points are connected, a moving average line is formed. Moving averages are most effective as trend-following tools. They smooth out the price action but incorporate a time lag. A moving average in a sideways moving market is less effective than a moving average applied to a trending market.

Formation: See *pattern*.

Fundamentals: Fundamental analysis assists in detecting which shares have a probability of increasing or decreasing in value based on the company balance sheet and profit/loss details. Economic supply and demand information is analysed rather than the market activity of price and volume action on a share chart.

Gaps: Gaps show that the price activity of the preceding period is completely above or below the next candlestick or bar apparent on the chart. Spaces or holes are left on the share chart when viewing candlestick charts or bar charts and these are called gaps. In Western analysis there are three main types of gaps: *continuation, breakaway* and *exhaustion*. A continuation gap suggests that the prevailing trend direction is likely to continue. An exhaustion gap is a gap that occurs after a trend which signals that the trend direction is likely to end. These can often be observed prior to a reversal trigger candlestick pattern. A breakaway gap usually signals the beginning of a new trend. These gaps can often confirm the new trend direction after a reversal trigger candle pattern.

Inside Day: A Western technical analysis term which implies that a trend reversal is likely. The range from the high to the low of the second period is totally within the trading span of the initial period. A harami candlestick pattern has similar qualities to this Western definition.

Island Reversal: An island reversal shows a small bar or multiple small bars, separated from the trading of the preceding and following sessions by significant gaps. This is a Western technical analysis term which suggests trend reversal.

Lead-up: The lead-up to a *trigger* candle consists of the activity of several of the preceding candles. For example, reversal patterns are only relevant if the share has already been trending, and will not be as appropriate for use while a share has been range-trading.

Line Chart: This type of chart connects the closing prices for each period to provide a continuous line that depicts share price action.

Long, or Going Long: This implies a bullish view of the market and describes when a trader purchases an instrument to initiate a transaction. When buying shares, traders have a long view of the market.

Long Candle: A candle showing a larger real body range than previous sessions on the chart.

Mid-Point: The mid-point is defined as being the 50% level of a candle's upper shadow to lower shadow range. It is typically used to describe a change in power from the bulls to the bears or vice versa. Usually, it is a more important concept when applied to shaven candles. The dark cloud cover and piercing pattern utilise this concept in the definition of these formations.

Momentum: The velocity of a price trend. These indicators show whether prices are declining or increasing at a faster or slower pace.

Moving Average: See *exponential moving average.*

Outside Day: This Western technical analysis term implies that a trend reversal is likely. The range from the high to the low of the second period totally engulfs the trading span of the first period. Bullish and bearish engulfing candlestick patterns have similar qualities to this Western definition.

Overbought: This term and the following term are normally used in relation to momentum indicators. An overbought line may be constructed manually by looking at the historic high points on a momentum indicator, or it may be an integral part of the indicator and shown as an indexed number from 0 to 100. When a momentum indicator has risen to a historic or indexed high, it implies an overbought condition whereby the instrument may be vulnerable to a sell-off.

Oversold: An oversold line may be constructed manually by looking at the historic low points on a momentum indicator, or it may be an integral part of the indicator and shown as an indexed number from 0 to 100. When a momentum indicator has dropped to a historic or indexed low, it implies an oversold condition whereby the instrument may be likely to rally.

Pattern: A single or a number of separate trading periods that form the data for a defined candlestick formation. If a single period forms the pattern, it is often called a one-line or single-line candlestick. Multiple candlesticks forming a pattern may be called two-line or double-line candles, etc.

Period: The time increment on a share chart. For example, a daily chart would show each candlestick to be composed of the open, high, low and close price for a day. The terms *session* and *period* are interchangeable.

Pullback: See *retracement*.

Put Option: A put option gives the buyer the right, but not the obligation, to sell a given security at a certain price within a given time.

Pyramid: To add equity to an existing trade that is trending in the expected direction.

Rally: An upward movement of prices.

Rate of Change (ROC): A momentum indicator with manually derived overbought and oversold conditions. Without a smoothing factor as shown by the *SIROC* indicator, the standard rate of change indicator can produce many whipsaws creating an abundance of buy and sell signals. It can be tricky to use effectively.

Real Body: The thick part of the candle representing the range between the opening price and the closing price. This is considered to be of more importance than the high and low prices for that period.

Resistance: A price level where sellers are expected to enter. It appears above the current price action and suggests that the price becomes resistant to making a higher high.

Retracement: A less significant version of a *correction*.

Reversal Patterns: The share price action is likely to change direction or soften into a sideways trading band after the appearance of a candlestick reversal pattern. Reversal patterns are more prevalent than continuation candlestick formations.

Session: See *period*.

Shadow: Shadows are the thin lines above and below the candlestick representing the extreme high and low for that session. The shadow provides an indication of buyer or seller strength.

Shadow Location: If there are long upper shadows at the top of an uptrend, this implies that the buyers have weakened and the sellers have begun to move in. If there are long lower shadows at the bottom of a downtrend, the price has dropped to a low enough level to encourage buyers to purchase the share.

Short, or Going Short: This implies a bearish view where traders short-sell the market, or sell to initiate a transaction. By selling shares and then purchasing them at a later date and a lower price, substantial profits can be made. Approximately 250 Australian shares can be short-sold.

Sideways Trend: A period of lateral price movement within a relatively narrow price range.

SIROC: Smoothed Indexed Rate of Change indicator. This smoothes the vagaries associated with a *Rate of Change* momentum indicator and provides a standardised and simpler interpretation.

Stop-Loss: A pre-determined price at which the trade is no longer performing as initially expected. Prudent traders keep their losses small by applying a stop-loss. The decision regarding where to position a stop-loss should be made prior to entering a trade. It is a strategy designed to protect a trader's equity. A time stop-loss suggests a pre-determined number of sessions is required in order for the instrument to trend in the expected direction, otherwise an immediate exit will be made. A trailing stop-loss is applied to a profitable trade in order to protect profits by moving the initial stop in the direction of the trend.

Support: A price level where buyers are expected to enter. It appears beneath the current market price and signifies that the price is resistant to making a lower low.

Tail: See *shadow*.

Technical Analysis: The use of price and volume action on a share chart to reach conclusions about the likely direction of future price activity.

Trigger Candle: This is the actual appearance of a reversal or continuation pattern. For a one-line candle, the trigger will be represented by one session only. For more complex two-line patterns, the trigger will consist of two sessions, etc.

Uptick: Any upward movement in price action. This upward movement can even be by the smallest price increment available on the price scale, e.g. one cent.

Uptrend: Prices are making consistently higher highs and higher lows.

Uptrend Line: A straight line is drawn in an upward left slanting angle connecting the troughs of the share price action. Once prices show evidence of dropping below this line in a sustainable manner, it is likely that the uptrend has been broken.

Volatility: A measure of fluctuation in market prices. Choppy shares with greater distances from the peak to the trough of the share price are more volatile and will produce a greater candle range.

Volume: The level of trading in a particular instrument. If volume increases in the direction of the trend or breakout, this adds to the weight of evidence that the share price movement is sustainable. For example, a volume increase on the uptrend provides support for a continuation of bullish activity.

White Candle: This candle shows a session where the closing price was higher than the opening price. This is inherently bullish.

Wick: See *shadow*.

Windows: See *gaps*.

Writing Options: Option writers collect a premium or fee from an option buyer and subsequently they are obligated to fulfil the demands of the option buyer. In relation to call options, the writer must *sell* their shares or have their shares 'called away' from them if the buyer decides to exercise the right. A put option writer is under obligation to *buy* the shares from a put option taker should the option be exercised.

INDEX

A

abandoned baby 68
All Ordinaries Index 125, 126, 129
Art of War, The 163
Australian Financial Review 153

B

back-testing 42, 163
bar chart 4, 8, 10
Beanie Babies 13
bearish continuation pattern 83
bearish engulfing pattern 43, 44, 45, 103
bearish rejection pattern 36-37
black candle 13-14, 141
black shooting star 103
body-to-body relationships 43, 53, 103
bottom reversal pattern 26, 27
bottom up analysis 125-126
breakaway gaps 94
breakout 126, 133, 136, 158
bullish engulfing pattern 44, 45-47, 133
bullish pattern 66, 133-134
bullish rejection pattern 37
bulls 12, 25

C

candle
—addition 16, 41-42, 44, 46, 163
—body size 16
—breakdown 41
—candle colours 10, 12, 15, 24
—development 16, 41-42
—history of 5-6
—range 15
—rules 161-164
—when to use them 14-15
change of polarity 110, 114
changes in behaviour 140
Chia, David 153-160
close 11
closing prices 118
colour of candles 10, 12, 15, 24
common doji 30
confirmation 17, 21, 22-23, 24, 45, 46,
    102, 122-123, 133, 134, 136, 137,
    140-142, 162
continuation gaps 93
continuation pattern 5, 14-15, 82-88, 158
crossovers 119, 121

D

dark cloud cover 49-50
data feed 159
day-trader 162
dead cross 118, 119, 123, 124
doji 30, 54, 119, 120
doji cross 30
dominant black candle 112-113
dominant candle 15, 34-36, 87
dominant white candle 110-111, 133,
    140, 141
downside tasuki gap 83
downtrending channel 101
downtrending gap 93
dragonfly 30

E

evening doji 68-71
evening star 63-66
ex-dividend gap 98
exhaustion gap 93
exiting a trade 157
expectancy rate 156
Exponential Moving Average (EMA) 119,
    120, 132

F

falling three method 87-88
formations 7
four-price doji 78
futures 5, 11, 157

G

gaps 22, 24, 49, 68, 83, 93-98, 123, 133,
    140, 141
golden cross 118, 119, 123, 124, 126
Gramza, Daniel 15-16, 41, 76
gravestone 30
gravestone doji 44

H

hammer 26-27, 67, 110
hanging man 29-30
harami 52-53
harami cross 30, 54-55
history of candlesticks 5-6

I

in-neck pattern 51
inside day 53
insignificant uptrend 56
Internet 144
intra-day candles 77
intra-day signals 144
inverted hammer 27-28
inverted hanging man 26
island reversal day 68

J

Japan 5-6
*Japanese Candlestick Charting
    Techniques* 7

L

lead-up 17, 21
line chart 9, 10
long candle 34-36
long white candle 127

M

market depth 115
Market Master 124, 126
*Martin Pring's Introduction to
    Candlestick Charting* 118
*Martin Pring's Introduction to Technical
    Analysis* 118
marubozu 33-34
mat-hold 85

medium-term investors 22
mid-points 110-111, 113
mobile phone 143
momentum 121-123
money management 76, 78
morning doji 68-71
morning star 66-68
moving averages 118-121, 123, 134, 135
multiple candlestick pattern 16, 22
multiple-line pattern 163
multiple lower shadows 107
Murphy, John J. 124

N

Nison, Steve 5

O

objectives 156
on-neck pattern 51
one-line rejection pattern 16-40
one-line reversal 21
open 11
opportunity cost 101
opportunity identification 136-139
opportunity pattern 76
options 5, 11, 47, 63, 98, 134
overbought line 121, 124
oversold line 121, 124

P

paging systems 143
patterns 7
piercing line 50
piercing pattern 50-51, 133, 141
piercing white line 50
placing orders 76, 77-78
position sizing 78
postdictive error 162
price rallies 104

Pring, Martin 118, 124
psychology 24-25, 27, 28, 29, 31, 45, 50, 52, 55, 79, 80, 158, 161
pullback 141
pyramiding 80, 158

R

raindrops 23
range-trading 132, 138
Rate of Change (ROC) 121
real body 10
real-time systems 144
rejection pattern 25, 36-37
Relative Strength Comparison (RSC) 124-125, 129
Relative Strength Indicator (RSI) 121, 122-123
resistance gaps 96-98
reversal pattern 5, 14-15, 21-37, 102, 132, 158, 161
Rice exchange 5
rickshaw man 30
rising three method 84, 85, 86
risk 80
rumours 11

S

searching procedures 142-144
Secret of Writing Options 63, 101
Secrets for Profiting in Bull and Bear Markets 135, 154
Sector Index 125
Seykota, Ed 157
shadows 10, 16
share stages 131-150, 158
ShareFinder Investment Services 125
shaven candle 33-34
shooting star 25-26, 29, 44
short candle 34
short-selling 98

short-term traders 22
significant numbers 115
single-line reversals 21
Smoothed, Indexed Rate of Change
    (SIROC) indicator 123-124
spinning top 33, 106
springs 110
Stochastic (STO) 121
Stone, Gary 125
stop-loss 79, 95, 98, 106, 141-142, 154
Sun Tzu 163
SuperCharts 143
support and resistance 96, 100, 102-103,
    127, 132, 133, 134, 141
support gap 95

T

tails 10
tasuki gap 95
Tate, Chris 80, 154
technical analysis 3, 7
Technical Analysis Explained 124
Tharp, Dr Van K. 79
three-line candle reversal pattern 62-72
three-river morning star 66
thrusting pattern 51
time increments 11-12, 159, 162
top down analysis 125
trading decisions 11
trading diary 81
Trading Your Way to Financial Freedom 79
training 155-156
trend direction line 72

trend reversal 5, 62
trendlines 72, 100, 102
trigger candle 93, 94, 161
triggers 17, 21, 22, 24, 25
Tulipomania 5
tweezer bottom 107-108
tweezer top 52, 96, 103-107
two crows 71-73
two-line reversal pattern 41-56

U

upside gap two crows 71
upside tasuki gap 82-83
upthrusts 109-110
uptrending gap 93

V

Visual Investor, The 124
volatility 11, 12
volume 12, 22, 133, 134, 140, 157

W

warrants 5, 98
watch list 143
Weinstein, Stan 135, 154, 158
Western techniques and candles
    117-129, 162
white candles 12-13, 123
wicks 10
windows 22, 93

www.tradingsecrets.com.au

Trading Secrets Pty Ltd provides a range of products and services to help maximise your trading profitability. Some of the products available via www.tradingsecrets.com.au are:

Candlestick Charting
Home Study Course

Share Trading 101
Triple Audio CD

Trading Psychology
Home Study Course

Leverage 101
Triple Audio CD

*The Secret of
Candlestick Charting*
Video Program

Psychology Secrets
Double Audio CD

*The Secret of
Candlestick Charting*
Poster

*The Secret of Pattern
Detection* Poster

Relaxation for Traders
Audio CD

Power Trading
Double Audio CD

Trading Secrets, 2nd ed

In *Trading Secrets*, 2nd ed, Louise Bedford shares more than 20 'secrets' she discovered on her way to becoming a successful trader. Practical review sections give you the chance to test your knowledge and cement essential principles. Newcomers to the market and more seasoned traders will find inspiration within these pages.

Charting Secrets

Given enough opportunities to practise your skills, you can become a successful trader. All you need to do is master the basics. Charting is a cornerstone skill for any trader. It can help you to visualise changes in the market so that specific trading rules can be developed. Learn the secrets of trend detection, set-ups and triggers, and the importance of a systematic approach to analysing market direction.

The Secret of Writing Options

More and more private investors and traders are entering the options market. Unlike a traditional investor, an options trader can still make money in a sideways-trending or falling market. *The Secret of Writing Options* is highly recommended for newcomers to options trading in Australia, and those already trading in the options markets. It starts with the basics, and discusses the discipline and attitude necessary to trade successfully.

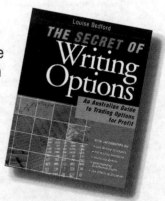

Trading Secrets, 2nd ed, *Charting Secrets* and *The Secret of Writing Options* are published by and available from Wrightbooks, an imprint of John Wiley & Sons Australia, Ltd.

Printed in Australia
06 Sep 2017
645502